From Preparation to Passion

**Devotional and Reflective Meditations
Celebrating the Lenten Season**

*Based On the Lectionary and Celebrated African
American Sacred Songs and Hymnody*

Eleanor Cooper Brown

From Preparation to Passion
Devotional and Reflective Meditations Celebrating the Lenten
Season Based On the Lectionary and Celebrated African American
Sacred Songs and Hymnody
by Eleanor Cooper Brown

Printed in the United States of America

ISBN 9781609577650

www.xulonpress.com

Preface

✿

Easter is coming and most people want to be ready for it. Moreover now as we live in the 21ˢᵗ century of "Common Era," preparations still mimic the influx of pagan cultural ideas that seeped into the holy traditions of the early church. In addition to being the Holiest of Days celebrated by the Church, Easter amongst non-believers also has become a secularized holiday, and particularly a commercialized one here in the United States. So what preparations do most Christians and non-Christians make? Shopping for new clothing often signifies the belief that Spring has arrived, and it is a time of renewal. Preparations for the Easter Egg Hunts and the Easter Ham for the Sunday dinner are high on the list too. Luxury vacations top the list of many who can well afford them. And for sure, there are many who stock up on chocolate, stuffed, electronic and live bunnies! However before Easter, pushing the worldly things aside, there should be some preparation for the Christian through the celebration of Lent.

Just as instituted by the early Christian Church, Lent for more than two thousand years now has been practiced as a season of preparation for Easter.

Traditionally, Lent marks the forty days before Easter, and is celebrated as a season of spiritual preparation in the Christian church. What does celebrating Lent mean to us today? The intent of observing Lent still as in the past is to provide new converts an opportunity to *prepare* through prayer and bible study for Holy Baptism. Others who have already been baptized prepare spiritually by either giving of themselves, or often giving up something that they really like, although they may find themselves over-indulging in that one thing by Easter Monday. Then too there are Christians who fast stringently for the forty days preparing their hearts and minds for a deeper sacred experience of the *passion*, crucifixion and resurrection of Jesus Christ our Savior. There are many devotions and books written to help communities of faith and individuals to observe the season of Lent in a devout manner. And here within is another resource that I hope will allow you to truly engage yourself in the *preparation* (bible study, prayer, and meditation) and propel you into a more Holy *passion* for Christ by the time we reach Easter. This push to a deeper passion may be realized and enhanced through the connection of the songs that perhaps you have grown to know as you've been on your Christian walk.

৪০০৪

Fact:
The focus of Lent was always threefold:

It was a time to prepare new converts for baptism through intensive classes and instruction.

It was a time for long-standing Christians to review their lives and renew their commitment to Jesus Christ.

It was a time for backsliders to be restored to the faith.

Source: http://wilstar.com/holidays/lent.htm

৪০০৪

Another objective of this Lenten devotional guide is to give you a focal point for committing to your own forty-day (actually 46 days*) regimen in preparation for Easter. As Lent begins each year on Ash Wednesday, a number of churches celebrate the beginning of Lent with the Ash Wednesday Service being held. This service allows congregants to come to the altar with prayers of repentance and to renounce the sins that may "so easily beset us." In many churches, the leaves of the Palms used to celebrate the previous year's Palm Sunday are kept and burned to produce the Ash. During the approach to the altar the minister or the priest will mark the sign of the cross on the forehead of each worshipper. The question is asked "Why ashes?" Symbolically in biblical times and following with Christianity, ashes represented mortality and repentance. We can associate the committal service of the departed human being, wherein the officiating clergy prays as dirt is being casted onto the coffin: "Ashes to Ashes, dust to dust," and further understand the symbolism of mortality. Correspondingly, if we think biblically, we read about many who under the weight of sin, placed themselves in ashes, or placed it on their heads and wore sackcloth as a means of confession, i.e. the king of Nineveh (Jonah3:6).

In the days following Ash Wednesday, we all will have the opportunity to focus on our personal disciplines and the sacrifices to which we commit. If none other, I would urge you to sacrifice the time to read daily the scripture(s) suggested before and after the meditation offered herein for every day of Lent. Here I also would like to share a past music ministry reflection as encouragement in asking ourselves where we would like to be post these 40 days in our spiritual walk. It was during the time of graduation for the Youth Choir high school senior members that we offered them a certificate on that commencement Sunday. The certificate contained the emblem of the mortarboard and the scroll and was entitled: *Graduate to a Higher Level of Faith!* The Romans 12:9-18 scripture was the printed message on the certificate. It was the message for their future conduct that we wanted them to take as they would be leaving our community of faith, and going away to college or some other life path. We adult choir leaders wanted to offer them some genuine words of encouragement to inspire them to increase their faith level as well as their academic level on their journey beyond that community of faith. For many of us, Lent can be a time to desire to graduate our faith to a higher level; it can be a time when we desire to delve deeper into the Holy things of God, pray more, fast more or even just be still in God's presence more.

Truly, it has been my personal experience that the messages of the sacred music during Lent, particularly including Holy Week, and up to Easter have

ഇ)രു

Fact:
There is evidence that Christians originally celebrated the resurrection of Christ every Sunday, with observances such as Scripture readings, psalms, the Eucharist, and a prohibition against kneeling in prayer. At some point in the first two centuries, however, it became customary to celebrate the resurrection specially on one day each year. Many of the religious observances of this celebration were taken from the Jewish Passover.
Source:
www.religionfacts.com/christianity/holidays/easter.htm

ഇ)രു

served as a tremendous means to sustain and enhance the study and meditation of the Word of God, as well as the corporate worship experiences. In these 46 days, we all should desire to immerse ourselves in listening to much Holy music while eliminating the "noise" of the world. We can let the message that the music brings seep deep down into our spirits, thus helping us to move perhaps to another level of prayer and praise.

With this in mind, I hope you enthusiastically will anticipate following this year's journey with me—*From Preparation to Passion*, and find this journey to be one that will join together the most exciting experience of God's Word and the sacred music which supports the Good News of the Resurrection of our Lord and Savior, Jesus Christ.

To God Be the Glory!

---

* Reason Lent Contains 46 Days: Each of the Sundays during lent are considered mini-Easters, so 6 days are added to the 40 days reserved for spiritual fasting.

Preparation through Prophecy

Ashes dried on the forehead, sins confessed in the hearts, minds, and souls of the worshippers, we tonight will move forward on our mission toward Easter. But I am reminded here to not forget that we as a people and a culture are in the midst of crisis!

"Blow the Trumpet, Sound the Alarm!"—are the words of the Prophet Joel! The Lord is in His Holy temple! Judgment day is drawing nigh. We are indeed a successive generation to this prophecy and the alarm is still clanging amidst the clamor of a somewhat over-cultured, highly intellectualized and technology-driven society.

Here I am reminded that my childhood religious experience was formed in the A.M.E. Church, where the hymns of the church and Negro Spirituals were the primary genre of sacred music being sung. The choirs, adult or children, may have sung any number of times the hymn: "Where Shall I Be?"[1] There is a pointed question this early church hymn queries throughout each line and on into the refrain: "O where shall I be when the first trumpet sounds? Where shall I be when it sounds so loud? When it sounds so loud as to wake up the dead, O Where shall I be when it sounds?"

The prophecy given by Joel and many of the prophets before and after him sounded the alarm indeed that the dead would wake up! Certainly in our times now, we prepare our hearts for the coming days when we celebrate Christ's resurrection from the dead. The New Testament scriptures do show us the fulfillment of Joel's prophecy. The scriptures also guide us to understand the lack of preparation, generally speaking, on the part of the people of Israel to receive their Messiah. Neither were they prepared for God's judgment. Reflecting on "Where Shall I Be?" it is interesting to notice that the theology of the hymn was remarkably in sync with the biblical theology of Joel's prophecy. The blow of the first trumpet (the *shofar*) was to warn of imminent danger! The second blowing was to gather the people together and call the nation to consecrate a fast—a call to penitence and remorse before God. The people of God were being mobilized to pray, no matter where or who they were: nursing babes or the bridegrooms. It was a call to everyone of every age. The prophetic call still rings today as each of us should be marshalling our congregations, young and old alike to come together in serious prayer for the impending dangers we face at this time in our communities, cities, nation, and world. Joel's message was to express to the people there was no other recourse but prayer.

Fasting and praying go hand in hand with Lent. We praise God because unlike the people of that time, we now have a Savior and Intercessor who is waiting to plead on our behalf. So we too should feel we have no other alternative but to "come boldly (*that is without reservation*) to the throne of grace, that we may obtain mercy and find grace to help" in this present time of need (Hebrews 4:14). Our society at its worse is in need of God's grace, and not the wrath of His Judgment. The question still looms in my mind from the song however, just in a little different way. Where shall we be in the coming weeks? Will we be closer to a crucified Savior? Will we be prepared for His waking up from the Dead? Where shall we be?

Ash Wednesday   **Reading: Joel 2:1-2, 12-17**

Your Study Notes Regarding Preparation and Prophecy

What preparations do you seek to make during Lent?

_____

_____

_____

_____

_____

_____

_____

_____

_____

_____

_____

_____

_____

_____

_____

_____

_____

_____

_____

_____

_____

Thursday—after Ash Wednesday   **Reading: Psalm 51:1-17**

Pain and a Cry for Relief

Often in life we may experience unwanted and sometimes unnecessary pain. This pain is the kind that throbs, lacking any pill that can cure it or make it subside. Habitually it may even be self-inflicted. It is the deep kind of pain that is perhaps much like what King David experienced after his grave self-inflicted error. *(2 Samuel 11:1-12:23)*

In January 2007, Daniel Benedict, former Worship Resources Director for the UMC General Board of Discipleship, entitled a worship website post: *"Kyrie Eleison"—A Prayer for When We Don't Know How to Pray.* The emphasis of his article centered on what *stand* Christians would take as then President Bush had, just hours before, outlined a plan for "victory/salvage in Iraq." Mr. Benedict posed the question "But what are we Christians to do?" And he proposed several answers; and one that specifically matched the title of his post. He wrote "…we could join the saints in praying or singing the ancient…Christian Greek prayer, *Kyrie eleison* (Lord, have mercy)." He went further to say, "It offers the church words with sufficient simplicity and depth to take us with our anguished world into the mercy of God."

How profound! Lord, Have Mercy! This prayer is a sure antidote that can remedy the hurt of "why this pain Lord?" "Lord, have mercy" is the cry for relief probably prayed most frequently by humankind, I would guess for the pains of life that really bore us down, and when we really *may not know* exactly how to pray. Our enslaved ancestors here in America, in all likelihood were not at all knowledgeable of the Greek *Kyrie eleison* chants, but their sufficiently simple faith passed on a tradition of praying *"Lord, have mercy"* in song, during camp meetings and later devotion services. These devotion services continue still today as the prelude to the worship service in many Baptist churches most notably and also is common in some other denominations. The singing of *"Lord, Have Mercy"* is a mournful chant sung in a minor key and what I would call an "uncommon" meter, denoting deep anguish, rising mid-song with a glimmer of tonal hope, yet a very simple plea of penitence. A leader calls out while the congregation joins in:

"Lord, have mercy,
Lord, have mercy
Lord, have mercy on my soul!
Lord, have mercy
Lord, have mercy
Lord, have mercy on my soul!"

Notice too that this simple prayer so resembles King David's minor key prayer of repentance as it starts in Psalm 51:1 —"Have mercy upon me, O God..." Within this Psalm we find his cry for relief from a throbbing pain. We find the prayer we easily can pray daily over the next 45 days, desirous of cleansing and communion with a Holy God. When we are hurting, and in deep pain, all we need is to just pray:" Lord, Have Mercy!" Amen.

Thursday—after Ash Wednesday   **Reading: Psalm 51:1-17**

Your Study Notes Regarding Pain

Today consider how often you say, consciously and unconsciously, Lord Have Mercy! Write down your thoughts.

_____

_____

_____

_____

_____

_____

_____

_____

_____

_____

೩)ೕೠ

Fact: Songs written in minor keys are melancholic. Songs written in major keys are happy songs. Try Singing "I Want Jesus to Walk With Me" and reflect on how you feel.
(Reference #563-African American Heritage Hymnal, GIA Publications, Inc.)

೩)ೕೠ

Friday—after Ash Wednesday   **Reading: 2 Corinthians 5:20b-6:10**

Almost Persuaded?

Christ calls each of us to be His ambassadors. Why? Well I heard one pastor put it like this in explaining the ambassadorship we have inherited: "We are now under new management." Exactly what was he saying? The Apostle Paul explained this thought to us in the sense that if we are in Christ then we are new creatures! What a great expression of what it means to be a Christian—under new management! Christ now manages our every movement, as it is now "in Him that we live and move and have our being." Under new management means we speak diplomatically on behalf of the top authorities of the Kingdom.

Here is how *The Message* by NavPress translates and suggests what our role should be as Christ's ambassadors:

> *"God has given us the task of telling everyone what He is doing. We're Christ's representatives. God uses us to persuade men and women to drop their differences and enter into God's work of making things right between them. We're speaking for Christ himself now: Become friends with God; he's already a friend with you."[2]*

God desires us to persuade people we know and don't know to make things right, not only with Christ, but also with each other. That's not an easy task; neither is the job of being an ambassador in the worldly sense. The work of persuading others on this journey can be a successful undertaking; yet there is also a probability of failure. Why? Because it is repentance on the part of the "wall-builders" that defines the decisive moment in reconciliation. Do you remember ever hearing the hymn *Almost Persuaded?* It's an older hymn which I think strikes a chord here in speaking to the difficulty we can encounter as emissaries for Christ.

"Almost persuaded, now to believe;
Almost persuaded Christ to receive:

15

Seems now some soul to say,' Go Spirit, go Thy way.'
Some more convenient day, on thee I'll call." [3]

These words express the reality that not everyone desires to hear the invitation to join God, nor to forgive or forget. Think on it, even the rich young ruler told Jesus, "some more convenient day!" Yet we are obligated to continue to carry out the job our executive administrator has given us. We know there will be victories if we persevere in telling others to "Become friends with God; he's already a friend with you". Today we should be challenged to speak this charge diplomatically to somebody who really needs to hear this message. The outcome and victory could be: "Persuaded"!

Friday—after Ash Wednesday   **Reading: 2 Corinthians 5:20b-6:10**

Your Study Notes Regarding Persuasion

Have you tried to persuade someone recently to come to Christ? What was the outcome? If you have not, write a list of several ways in which you can try to be a better ambassador for Christ today.

_____

_____

_____

_____

_____

_____

_____

_____

_____

_____

_____

_____

_____

_____

_____

_____

_____

_____

Saturday—after Ash Wednesday　　　　**Reading: Matthew 6:1-6, 16-21**

God-Pleasing Piety

Growing up in a rural country setting offered many opportunities to visit a number of churches with my grandmother in the various communities of our county. At some special fundraising services like the Harvest Festivals, the "collection" was a celebrated event aimed at meeting a specific goal. If the actual giving was lower than expected, there might be preachers, or church deacons or trustees that would hawk for more! "Come on, we've got to raise a thousand dollars tonight. Can I get all who can give fifty to come on up right now! Can you give twenty-five dollars? Ten, five; come on up and give a dollar! We need to make this collection up before we leave!" Then there were often men of local status, who might come forward and offer to make up the difference in what was collected and the goal! "Oh, thank you Sir" the pastor might respond. Often this person could be talked about for the following week, no matter whether their intent was to receive praise or not. The "calling out" setting itself was a forum for bringing attention to any giver. You see these were also times when rural Black churches lacked detailed knowledge of enveloped giving.

Being "called out" for our benevolent acts is not something we should wish for or take pleasure in. Jesus tells us to forget the pretentiousness in our giving, praying and fasting! That type of role-play doesn't please God. We are encouraged to replace posturing with dependency. God sees, and knows what we need. The state of our devotion and reverence in giving, praying and fasting is more important than the magnitude of what we need outwardly display.

In the text of the song "*God Is*," Dr. Robert J. Fryson expressed God-pleasing piety simply as "I've got to fast and pray, stay in the narrow way."[4] Jesus admonishes that giving, praying and fasting in the "narrow way" are devout but personal acts of worship. The passageway that the woman at the treasury walked with only two mites *(Mark 12:41-44)* perhaps was narrowed, yet a committed way. The path to the cross for Jesus was a narrow way, although God had already spoken that "in Him I am well pleased." Let us focus today and in the days following on "staying in the narrow way" without fanfare, but in humble solitude. This will be pleasing to God!

Saturday- after Ash Wednesday **Reading: Matthew 6:1-6, 16-21**

Your Study Notes Regarding God Pleasing Piety

What are some things you have learned in your life about piety?

_____

_____

_____

_____

_____

_____

_____

_____

_____

_____

_____

_____

_____

_____

_____

_____

_____

_____

_____

_____

_____

_____

_____

First Sunday in Lent   **Reading: Mark 8:31-38**

The Paradox of More and Enough

"The ideal is to pray for enough possessions to avoid the temptation to steal but not enough to feel independent of God." – Dr. Bloomberg of Baker House Bible Dictionary

When is enough, enough? It was 2009 and the headlines reported that "Wall Street continues either to tumble or rollercoaster." Greed has been the catchword of the decade! For what then does it profit those who gain more and more, in exchange for their own soul? The Ponzi scheme is a renewed and commonly heard term these days. Prior to the arrest of Bernard Madoff, the term Ponzi may have been familiar only to those in higher finance markets. You will find the name of the scheme derived from a man by that same name, Charles Ponzi, an Italian emigrant to America, who once was described as "one of the greatest swindlers in American history." His schemes brought in so much cash, he was said to be pulling in $250,000 a day back in 1920. But then as the plot collapsed, he was indicted, prosecuted, jailed and deported back to Italy. It must be noted however that this man Ponzi spent the last years of his life in poverty. After having suffered a stroke, being blind in one eye, and partially paralyzed, he died in a charity hospital. It would appear from historical accounts that with no apparent remorse during his last hospital interview he claimed: "It was easily worth fifteen million bucks to watch me put the thing over!"

Jesus saw the need to teach His disciples and all who would follow in their way to pray: "Lead us not into temptation, but deliver us from evil." Deliver us from the "root of all evil" should be the catchwords now to counter the decades of greed in America. These are perilous times in which it is so important to latch on to the instructions of Jesus to pray for deliverance from evil and moreover, the evil one. "*In times like these*"[5] we really do need a Solid Rock like Jesus, to hold on to, so that we avoid temptations such as those of Ponzi and his subsequent imitators. Clearly these may have been people who obviously thought *more* was better. We too can pray asking for deliverance from wanting so much *more* than we truly need!

Coming out of the wilderness after forty days of fasting, "all the kingdoms of the world and their glory" was the *"more"* Satan offered Jesus. Just like Jesus, rebuking the tempter, we should choose to deny the worldly rewards that are so often flashed before us, and understand more about the path of sacrifice. Worldly "kings and kingdoms will all pass away,"[6] but the Kingdom of God offers eternal rewards. Amassing worldly goods is only temporal gain *(more)* which risks eternal loss. Choosing greater works, all for the sake of Christ, we truly gain all things eternal *(enough)*. *Selah!*

First Sunday in Lent   **Reading: Mark 8:31-38**

Your Study Notes Regarding the Paradox of More and Enough

Express in your own words what Jesus says about the paradox of more and enough.

_____

_____

_____

_____

_____

_____

_____

_____

_____

_____

_____

_____

_____

_____

_____

_____

_____

_____

Monday—after the 1st Sunday in Lent   **Reading: Psalm 25:1-10**

Patiently Waiting

Generally speaking, what impact does waiting for something to happen have on your state of mind?

My paternal grandmother passed away, now some 30 years ago. Within a few days after her death, on her bedroom dresser I found her Bible turned to Psalm 40. Since I was living away from home at the time of her passing, I wondered if she had asked someone to read this Psalm to her during her last days. As I read the first few lines, it was with a dismayed, but instinctive perception that I understood perhaps this was her prayer and testimony during such an unexpected illness and the approaching transition. It has taken me all these years now to grasp the profound wisdom of what was then not so obvious.

Certainly waiting for God is a virtue. Waiting for God to do what God will do in His own time is an even more desirable discipline for all of us to constantly cultivate. Our highly developed society sometimes mandates we be creatures of haste. More often than not, we tend to want to rush things along. Sometimes however, like my grandmother, more recently my father, and the many other souls who have come to the threshold of eternity, there are limited choices for cultivating that virtue of waiting. Waiting in sickness is considerably different than waiting in health.

Yet, in our healthiness, if we desire to develop a passion for spiritual patience, there are steps we can take on our journey to Easter Sunday. First, we should daily wait in His presence for direction. There are points in the scriptures where either psalmists, prophets or the saints may ask "How long O Lord" must we wait? The Psalmist in 25:5 answers "I wait on you all the day." In His presence, quietly engulfed in His Spirit, is the sense of this type of waiting. While waiting in this atmosphere of expectation, we easily can be stirred to move into a deeper worship of God.

Secondly, we should wait in a state of continual trust. Knowing that no matter where we are, at all times and in all places, God will deliver us with his enduring mercy. In this position, our confidence cannot be shaken. We then can sing with utmost assurance, "Blessed Assurance!...I in my Savior am happy and blest, watching and waiting, looking above, filled with his goodness, lost in his love.

On the other hand, the sick and weary soul that yearns for God to "Call Death," as James Weldon Johnson so penned it[7], certainly might ask "how long?" and may humbly answer *"My soul waits for the Lord more than those who watch for the morning— Yes, more than those who watch for the morning." (Psalm 130:6)*

Matthew Henry's commentary clarifies this type of waiting in sickness further by saying, "I wait for the Lord; from him I expect relief and comfort, believing it will come; longing till it does come, but patiently bearing the delay of it, and resolving to look for it from no other hand. *My soul doth wait*; I wait for him in sincerity and not in profession only. ... it is for the Lord that my soul waits, for the gifts of his grace and the operations of his power...*more than those that watch for the morning, [those]* who are well-assured that the morning will come; and so am I, that God will return in mercy to me, according to his promise;"[8]

We will find, whether in sickness or in health, a number of thoughts on waiting until a specific change comes in our lives can put us in some serious modes of deep contemplation. Let's each meditate during these days of Lent, on how patiently waiting for God, waiting in His presence, where we are right now, will prepare us for the deliverance Christ's resurrection truly promises.

Monday—after the 1st Sunday in Lent   **Reading: Psalm 25:1-10**

Your Study Notes Regarding Patience

Consider how many ways in which you can practice waiting on God for the right answer to a problem?

_____

_____

_____

_____

_____

_____

_____

_____

_____

_____

_____

_____

ഐരു

Suggested Song for
Worship: "Time in Praise"
(All Day Long, I've been
with Jesus) Recorded by the
Gospel Music Workshop of
America (GMWA) Women of
Worship.

ഐരു

Tuesday—after the 1st Sunday in Lent   **Reading: 1 Peter 3:18-22**

Heavy Precipitation

Didn't it rain! Noah's message fell on many deaf ears! Only Noah and seven others, his wife, three sons, and their wives were saved from the great flood; saved by God's grace. The disobedient, "the rebellious, un-persuadable, and unbelieving"[9] aggravated God's patience. It seems though there was enough time for repentance, as it took Noah about 120 years to build the ark! But yet the Bible tells us that "Their bodies were drowned, and their spirits" were cast into the prison of hell. And for forty days and nights you might say there was for the earth a Baptism by water that would save future generations from such wrath.

From a different perspective however, meditate on the way the message of the flood was understood in the language of the African American slave or their descendents in song. Here's the way they told the story:

O Didn't It Rain (Negro Spiritual)

Fo'ty days fo'ty nights
When de rain kept a-fallin',
De wicked clumbd de tree,
An' for help kept a-callin',
For they heard de waters wailin'
Didn't it rain, rain
Didn't it rain,

Tell me Noah, didn't it rain
Some clim'd de mountain,
Some clim'd de hill,
Some started sailin'
An' a-rowin' wid a will;
Some tried swimmin'
An' I guess they're swimmin' still,
For they heard de waters roarin'
Didn't it rain, rain, didn't it rain,

Tell me Noah, didn' it rain,
Didn' it rain [10]

There are still heavy rainstorms that fall all over the world in our times today. The resulting floods cause loss of life, and at times devastate lives beyond repair. Despite rescue and recovery, a lifetime of worldly possessions and irreplaceable memories are washed away. And it brings us to wonder, is God trying to tell us something?

So intriguingly enough, we find the Apostle Peter gives us another perspective to think on deeply about those "deaf ears" that according to our ancestors had "clim'd," and were "arowin' and swimmin'." In addressing the days of Noah, Peter points out that God in his longsuffering, waited patiently 120 years; and yet all those same very wicked souls which were cast into the prison then, were there, present and accounted for, when Jesus after His death and in the Spirit by which "He was raised to life" (1 Peter 3:19), descended into hell to preach God's salvation. Oh what a foretaste of glory divine! Incorporating here the words of another Apostle, Paul, we all are urged to "think on these things!" (Philippians 4:8) *Selah!*

Prayer for today: During these forty days, save us Lord from that kind of rain, we pray. Amen.

Tuesday—after the 1st Sunday in Lent   **Reading: 1 Peter 3:18-22**

Your Study Notes Regarding Precipitation

Has there been any "rain" in Your Life? What do you understand to be the central message of the scripture noted here today?

_____

_____

_____

_____

_____

_____

_____

_____

_____

_____

_____

_____

_____

_____

_____

_____

_____

_____

_____

_____

_____

Power Worth Having!

"Have you got good religion? Cert'nly Lord!"
"Have you been redeemed? Cert'nly Lord!"
"Have you been to the water? Cert'nly Lord!
"Have you been baptized? Cert'nly Lord!
"Cert'nly, Cert'nly, Cert'nly Lord!"[11]

These stanzas come from a traditional spiritual that was a favorite of one of my former choir members, Mr. James Cherry. He sang with the Mens' Gospel Choir at Russell Memorial CME Church in Durham, North Carolina where he was, as far as I know, a dedicated and lifelong member. During my time spent as a musician in this church, I learned the "Cert'nly Lord" song which is built on a vocal genre of call and response. Mr. Cherry, an aging senior at that time, would call out "Have you got good religion" with a serious tenor voice of conviction, as the men behind him would answer in strong response, "Cert'nly Lord!" However, their rendition of the spiritual had an improvised chorus not found in the *Songs of Zion* version that moved to:

"If you have that old time religion,
If you have that old time religion,
If you have that old time religion,
Then you ought to show some sign,
You ought to walk right,
you ought to talk right
You ought to pray right,
Then you ought to stay right!
Cert'nly, Cert'nly, Cert'nly Lord!"

This rendition of the spiritual truly expresses the essence of the power of baptism in one's life!

"Cert'nly Lord!" If you've been baptized you ought to show some sign! Look at what happened when Jesus went to the water: The heavens were torn apart and the Spirit of God descended in the form of a dove; and God spoke! What a sign! That's power worth having! And did Jesus subsequently go about showing that with His baptism He was now empowered? Indeed He did! Although we know he was sinless, His obedience to baptism was to position himself among sinners as His work of salvation still lay ahead. With Baptism He was empowered to withstand forty days in the wilderness, the subsequent temptations and then He went forward with His divine Ministry—starting in his home town, Nazareth. There he proclaimed the power to preach, power to heal, power to proclaim and power to transform! That was some sign, and power worth having!

You know, as I think of it, Mr. Cherry showed a sign that he was baptized with Holy Spirit power! A gentle and kind man He was, always serving faithfully, never missing an opportunity to open prayer meeting on Wednesday nights or the Power Prayer Pool on Saturday mornings or taking special care of the sanctuary. Yes, with baptism comes Holy Spirit power. If we've been baptized, let's pray for an increase of the Holy Spirit in our lives today, which is the kind of power that is worth having! For those who yet have not been to the water, well be assured, there is power worth having awaiting you! To God Be the Glory!

Wednesday—after the 1st Sunday in Lent   **Reading: Mark 1:9-15**

Your Study Notes Regarding Holy Spirit Power

Have you been baptized? If yes, describe some of your Holy-Spirit powered moments. If no, plan a course of action you need to take to become baptized.

_____

_____

_____

_____

_____

_____

_____

_____

_____

_____

_____

_____

_____

_____

_____

_____

_____

_____

_____

Thursday—after the 1st Sunday in Lent   **Reading: Psalm 32**

Pardoning Power

Surely, God is Able! A song of this title emerged from the gospel tradition in the African-American Church. I'm almost certain it is probably a song our grandparents and great-grandparents would have known in the '50s and '60s. In our times right now, it is probably not even familiar to many older or younger generation churchgoers. You see, Rev. Herbert Brewster, D.D. of Memphis, Tennessee, a pastor, great songwriter and "distinguished pulpit and radio personality," wrote hundreds of gospel songs like this one. It was made famous by Clara Ward and the famous Ward Singers.[12] Quartets, much like the Five Blind Boys of Mississippi, gospel singers, and choirs alike may have sung many variations of this melody to instruct their listeners that our "God is able to carry you thro," God is able to protect in time of trouble, and "help us carry, our heavy load." "Yes God is Able!"

Let's flash back centuries before Christ, and we will find King David was a gospel songwriter of sort, in that in writing psalms for temple worship he would label each with the suggested or appropriate delivery for the occasion. His message in Psalm 32, while labeled for much contemplation and instruction, illustrates too the power repentance brings when one knows, "surely God is able" to pardon sins. You see King David's soul was deeply troubled, and he had kept very silent about his sin! Before his day of atonement with Nathan the Prophet, His insides were literally being eaten up (*2 Samuel 12:1-13*)! In this Psalm, however, it is from His own experiences that King David concluded a need for others to be instructed that sins can be forgiven, and to understand the ensuing joy that then can lead the pardoned one to praise of God for his steadfast love. J. Clinton McCann Jr. substantiates this thought about this Psalm as he writes: "From the first five verses, it is clear that the psalmist's confession of sin has been a cathartic [*therapeutic*], healing experience. But from the subsequent verses, it is just as clear that the psalmist's attention is focused not upon himself or herself. Rather, the psalmist immediately directs attention to others and to God." [13]

33

Now let's fast forward. Certainly when we come to points in our lives where we know we need to confess our sins, we too desire to feel fully God's pardoning grace. Sin can be a heavy load even upon the most insensate or hardened of hearts. Here is where God is able to step in and forgive unconditionally. Then in a similar way, just like King David, our testimony of liberation from the load having been lifted is one we want others to know. We want to tell them, "Yes God is able!" We also can't thank God enough!

Whether the testimony is written in poetry, like the Psalms, or a gospel song, such as Rev. Brewster's, or a simple hand-written note to a friend, the sum effect is, somebody can be advised to know God's pardoning grace brings peace. It brings joy. It brings renewal of one's physical being! So as we move about work, home or play, let us tell somebody who really needs to know today, that "Surely, God is Able" to carry you through—whatever may be troubling you!

Thursday—after the 1st Sunday in Lent   **Reading: Psalm 32**

Your Study Notes Regarding Pardoning

Is it easy for you to forgive others? Write your thoughts about forgiveness.

_____

_____

_____

_____

_____

_____

_____

_____

_____

_____

_____

_____

_____

_____

_____

_____

_____

_____

_____

Friday—after the 1st Sunday in Lent   **Reading: Romans 5:12-19**

The Parallel –Death and Life

For since by man came death, by Man also came the resurrection of the dead. For as in Adam all die, even so in Christ all shall be made alive. –1 Corinthians 15:21-22

This 1Corinthians 15 scripture is so elaborately woven into the music of a venerable and grand Easter Cantata, "No Greater Love" by John W. Peterson.[14] The music with these words offers a stirring passage found in the finale of the cantata. The passage most powerfully precedes the *conjunction* that coordinates the phrase that defines an ultimate division in time for all of mankind: "**But,** now is Christ Risen, Hallelujah, Hallelujah—risen from the dead! " This passage moves the parallel of man's death in Adam, and life in Christ.

The Apostle Paul perhaps chose to explain to his hearers that indeed there was a parallel worth noticing. In the book of Romans he summed it up in a few words as "all have sinned and fall short of the Glory of God" (Romans 3:23) to parallel the death that comes by Adam. Adam's sin brought to man mortality. The Glory of God is immortality. So Christ, Son of Man, the second Adam, a parallel in a sense, would bring to man immortality. The first Adam is explained as "the representative head of mankind in their fall." The second Adam in the person of Christ is "the representative head of mankind in their recovery."[15]

Yes we are all frail beings by the nature of Adam, but when we are in the nature of Christ our being rests on a solid and firm foundation. As we look forward to celebrating the death and resurrection of Christ these two millennia and more, let us not forget to consider that in Christ, there was no greater love, as He laid down His life so that each of us would have a right to recovery! With Adam and sin, mankind lost immortality. Jesus Christ's life, death and resurrection were in a sense, a rescue mission to get it back. Praise God! Moreover, his work is not done as Jesus will come again to rescue us from the wrath that is yet to come.

The beauty of the music and words of an Easter cantata such as *"No Greater Love"* also reminds us to consider another parallel— the relationship of God the Father and Jesus Christ the Son. Yes it was no greater love than the agape love of God as the Father who so loved the world. He gave His only begotten Son, so that whoever would believe in Him would not experience eternal death, but would in Christ have immortal life—that is, everlasting life. Oh what a parallel! The greater love of the Father for the world! The Greater Love of the Son who would lay down His Life so that grace would abound. It is no wonder that John Peterson and other song writers through the ages would be led to exclaim: "Hallelujah! Hallelujah! Let us shout with Joy too: Hallelujah! Hallelujah!

Friday—after the 1st Sunday in Lent   **Reading: Romans 5:12-19**

Your Study Notes Regarding the Parallels of Life and Death

Today, write about some of your thoughts on life and death?

_____

_____

_____

_____

_____

_____

_____

_____

_____

_____

_____

_____

_____

_____

_____

_____

_____

_____

_____

_____

_____

_____

_____

_____

Saturday—after the 1st Sunday in Lent   **Reading: John 10:11-15**

Pursuing Jesus

Recently I read a blogger's comment about the song, *"Take Up Your Cross"* by the Brooklyn Tabernacle Choir[16] Interestingly the writer said "it is a very encouraging song especially to the Christian believers who don't want to be identified by Christ." Wow! Consider that many who say "I believe", struggle with the identification of being Christ-like. That is certainly an anomaly.

A Kingdom Dynamics meditation on Sacrifice tells us that "Growing in the likeness of Christ requires that we be willing to lay down our lives, and take up our cross daily."[17] Indeed the path of sacrifice in following Christ is not an easy road to walk, but as the meditation concludes that "when we sacrifice for Him, <u>that</u> opens the way for His life to reveal even more of the glory of His way and will"— and for each of us to "discover new dimensions of eternal love and liberty."

So I agree with the blogger on the one point of encouragement. Being followers of Christ unquestionably is the principal criterion of being a Christian. So Yes! The message of the song indeed is encouraging because it urges us to earnestly choose to identify with Christ as we pursue Him. It encourages us to make the sacrifices, often at the cost of losing friends and material things but gaining things eternal. The song encourages us to follow Jesus regardless of the loss of our own identity. We should never be ashamed to be called one of His followers. So today while meditating on how much Jesus did for us as the Apostle John records in this reading, let's reflect on these words of *"Take Up Your Cross."*

"Take up your cross and follow Jesus,
Take up your cross, every day.
Don't be ashamed to say that you know him,
Count the cost, take up your cross and follow him.
What are you doing for the king
have you really given everything
for the one who gave his all for you?

39

Don't be satisfied just to know
that the Lord has saved your soul
have you forgotten what you need to do?
Don't be ashamed to say that you know him
count the cost, take up your cross and follow him

I know sometimes the road is long
and I know sometimes you feel like you can't go on
but you can make it, you just,
Don't be ashamed to say that you know him
count the cost, take up your cross and follow him."

Saturday—after the 1st Sunday in Lent Reading: John 10: 11-15

Your Study Notes Regarding Pursuing Jesus

List some specific commitments you need to make to follow Jesus while claiming His identity.

_____

_____

_____

_____

_____

_____

_____

_____

_____

_____

_____

_____

_____

_____

_____

_____

_____

_____

_____

Second Sunday in Lent   **Reading: Luke 13:31-35**

No Need for Phobia or Panic

Toward the mid 90's there was a catchphrase created as a clothing trademark name which brandished the words "No Fear!" The company marketed T-shirts initially with slogans that hyped the worth of the more dangerous sports such as motocross, windsurfing, and other environmentally hazardous pursuits. From this onset came another round of popular clichés that piggy-backed the *No Fear* concept which included phrases on T-Shirts like "Ain't skeered," "Not skeered" or "I'ain't skeered!"

When I consider these specific tags that modern youth have worn and made into time tested sayings, I also think Jesus Himself could have been an original author of "Ain't Skeered" -but in Aramaic that is. The account that Luke relates about the Pharisees coming to Jesus[18] and saying essentially: "Get out and go away from here, because Herod wants to kill you!" is the backdrop for Jesus' retaliatory mocking of them to say as much as –"I ain't skeered." Afraid, terrified? That might have been the state of Herod's guilt-ridden insecurity since he had been the key perpetrator in the just recent and most heinous crime of beheading John the Baptist! You see John had called Herod out for adulterous incest.

With a great deal of irony and satire, Jesus replied to these deceptive warnings of the Pharisees for his safety by putting things in a true order; it was an order of how he planned to calmly and without fear of Herod accomplish his mission. I would say lightheartedly that Jesus wanted these leaders and Herod to know: *Verily* I say unto you, "I ain't skeered."

Take note in Luke's text however that Jesus spoke as a Prophet, so he was at liberty to call Herod out in his tarnished kingship: "That Fox!" He called him. To illustrate this point further, think back on the prophet Nathan when he told King David something like: "You're da man David; you took the Lamb!" Secondly Jesus also spoke as the King of Kings, since all authority under Heaven was His; so rightfully, He could usurp Herod's threats! As a prophet He knew and mockingly jabbed that prophets were killed—that is, were stoned to death—only in Jerusalem. So Jesus let Herod know, I'm moving on from Galilee deliberately "today, and tomorrow, and the day following," and I will be out of your jurisdiction Herod! I'm headed to Jerusalem. Besides in Jerusalem a true prophet was always indicted and prosecuted as a false prophet anyway. So Jesus had no fear because He knew what was to come already.

The good news is that we too now know what was to come in Jerusalem. During this Lenten journey, if we would reach back into the Songbook of Israel, we would find a great creed to support us when we come up against schemes and snares such as Jesus discerned. Also when we face such evils of fear linked to loneliness, depression, unemployment, loss of love or even poverty, the Psalmist offers us words to position deep within our hearts an unflinching fortitude in these uncertain times; we don't have to brandish a T-shirt to hype our conviction. With resolve all we need is to just declare:

The Lord is my light and my salvation; whom shall I fear?
The Lord is the strength of my life; of whom shall I be afraid? -Psalm
27:1

Many of us have sung these words to a contemporary tune arranged by Lillian Bouknight.[19] Whenever singing this tune again, think of Jesus as he said "I will be casting out demons, and healing people;" doing good things "Mr. Herod"–thus translated: "I ain't skeered!" Jesus set His face to complete that journey to Jerusalem. There is where He, the true prophet, Son of Man and Son of God, although falsely prosecuted and slain, ultimately became our Salvation, so that we too have no need to be "skeered."[20]

Ask somebody today "are you skeered" about anything? If so, let them know God has not given us a Spirit of fear, but He has given us a Savior, Christ Jesus! Tell them there is no need to fear! Tell them, "Don't be afraid! Don't be "skeered"! Jesus wasn't."

Second Sunday in Lent   **Reading: Luke 13: 31-35**

Your Study Notes Regarding No Need for Panic

Think of times when words of others were meant to intimidate or deceive you. Write here how you responded. What can you do differently from today on to thwart similar pretenses or threats in the future?

_____

_____

_____

_____

_____

_____

_____

_____

_____

_____

_____

_____

_____

_____

_____

_____

_____

_____

Monday – after the 2nd Sunday in Lent   **Reading: Psalm 22:23-31**

Filled in His Presence

Jesus made it clear as he declared his mission: He came to seek the lost sheep of the house of Israel. But yet He was equally compelled to mingle with the likes of the Samaritan woman at the well. He traveled to regions like Tyre and Sidon where the Canaanite woman challenged the priority of His Messianic mission. He marveled at the faith of persons like the centurion with a sick servant, who undoubtedly believed in His omnipresence, and He sat at the table of sinners and ate with them, ministering to their needs.[21]

In His presence *the poor and needy were satisfied* with more than they could physically eat or probably understand, and most assuredly one would think that each experienced a new and unique fullness of spiritual joy. Many who encountered Jesus along the way left His presence with much loud thanksgiving and exuberant praise. Even on the cross, a distinct fullness of being in His presence was realized by the thief who cried "Lord, remember me" seeing that Jesus guaranteed him a place in Paradise that day.[22] In his walk, Jesus ministered to the poor and needy who lived in desperation or had been abandoned by the "righteous" house of Israel. Many of these folks were like the banished lepers, or the man at the Pool in Bethsaida that had no one to help him into the water. They were the sick who needed a physician! Ultimately, Jesus knew too that He would be abandoned and forsaken. Still, in His humanity, Jesus *was* the "bread and the cup" personified, as He intimately spoke and touched the lives of these people dismissing their sin and leaving them with an occurrence that would most likely be etched on their minds forever, always remembering Him.

Richard Blanchard may have connected with the thought of Jesus being that physical "bread and wine" when he was inspired to write the words,

Fill My Cup, Lord, I lift it up, Lord, Come and quench this thirsting of my soul;

Bread of Heaven, feed me till I want no more—
Fill my cup, fill it up, and make me whole![23]

We thank God that even though Jesus was abandoned and forsaken on a cross of redemption, drinking from a bitter cup, taking on the sin of all, Jews and Gentiles alike, we can praise Him forever for that victory. With His disciples, He took the time to prepare an everlasting "service of the table" so that in His presence, we too may be sufficiently filled. As Jesus has always promised to be with us we are always in His presence.

Today offers us another opportunity to pray "Fill my cup Lord," minister to our needs Lord. And upon being filled, like the many who experienced His presence, we too with a loud voice can glorify God, giving Him thanks; giving Him praise! Amen! Amen!

Monday – after the 2nd Sunday in Lent   **Reading: Psalm 22:23-31**

Your Study Notes Regarding Jesus' Presence in Your Life

Make note of the times that you have experienced the fullness of Jesus' presence in your life.

_____

_____

_____

_____

_____

_____

_____

_____

_____

_____

_____

_____

_____

_____

_____

_____

_____

_____

_____

_____

Tuesday – after the 2nd Sunday in Lent   **Reading: Romans 4:13-25**

God's Promises, Abraham's Pattern

If those who get what God gives them only get it by doing everything they are told to do and filling out all the right forms properly signed, that eliminates personal trust completely and turns the promise into an ironclad contract! That's not a holy promise; that's a business deal. –The Message, Romans 4:14

"I Trust in God, wherever I may be, upon the land or on the rolling sea! For come what may, from day to day, my heavenly Father watches over me!"[24]

Until recently the words of this song have always been a comfort and a testimony as I have yearned to walk in the spirit of faith and trust. However, at the present, hauntingly so, I am compelled to internalize more deeply these ideals brought forward in these words, taking complete confidence in God's covenant promises to know that if He watches over the sparrow, surely He knows all of the things I need. You see it was just a short while ago, I personally confessed the trust I have in God through this song to my fellowship of faith, and just within the next day or so, calamity happened. Then the question pointed at me was "How do you handle trust in the midst of tragedy?" Does trust just go out the window, when your world seems upside down? Or does trust remain confident residing in a maximum security compartment of your mind, body and soul?

Amongst the great cloud of faith witnesses roll-called by the Hebrews writer, we find Abraham. He trusted God to do what God said He would do. He also believed that despite his and Sarah's inabilities, God could change things. And God did! Abraham saw God to be "greater than his inabilities." Here is an example of his stated faith in God: *"By faith, Abraham, at the time of testing, offered Isaac back to God. Acting in faith, he was as ready to return the promised son, his only son, as he had been to receive him—and this after he had already been told, "Your descendants shall come from Isaac." Abraham figured that if God wanted to, he could raise the dead. In a sense, that's what happened when he received Isaac back, alive from off the altar."*[25]

My shattering experience was too the loss of an only son! Not mine, but my brother's only offspring. So suddenly, unexpectedly, and so brutally, he died. To me, it seemed so symbolic of a sacrificial lamb that lay at the altar. Any mother, father, sister or brother, might feel the same way. In the weakness of this moment I did not want to let go. There was no ram in the thicket here. So many questions came of why and what unseen forces prevailed. But I had to give all of the hurt and pain and resulting remorse over to God, during these days of despair. There is no human reckoning logic that understands such a senseless act of violence. And in trying to find answers to why this sorrowful thing had to happen, we understand that it is only a divine reckoning that will ever make that exactly clear to each one of us: mother, sister, grandmother, aunts, uncles, cousins or friends –all who truly loved him. God's truth will always triumph over evil. The disposition of such grief also pushed the button to sound the alarm that my trust and faith in God and His divine intervention in this violent act has to remain secure otherwise it is not faith but pretense.

So I must continue to sing, "I trust in God, wherever I may be…" I must prefer to follow Abraham's pattern knowing that God is greater than any circumstance. Trusting God says that the life and death of this only son, this sacrificial lamb so to speak was somehow a part of a greater redemption. Knowing God's promises are unbreakable, I too know that He promised, if we are in Christ, then we all will be made alive; so when He comes with "trumpet sound," we know that the dead in Christ will rise, first.

Let us all praise God for His promises! Let us pray for strength to be obedient as we grow, trusting God more for all things.

Prayer: Dear Lord, please let your Holy Spirit guide us continually to trust you in all of life's circumstances. We pray to trust you to be our refuge and strength, a very present help in our times of trouble. In our weakest moments, help us always to feel and trust in your all-sufficient strength and your steadfast mercy. Amen!

Tuesday—after the 2ⁿᵈ Sunday in Lent   **Reading: Romans 4:13-25**

Your Study Notes Regarding Promises and Patterns

How are you trusting God's promises and following Abraham's pattern? Who has been a role model for you to follow in your life?

_____

_____

_____

_____

_____

_____

_____

_____

_____

_____

_____

_____

_____

_____

_____

_____

_____

_____

_____

_____

Wednesday—after the 2ⁿᵈ Sunday in Lent   Reading: Genesis 17:1-7, 15-16

Patriarchal Promises

A traditional Negro spiritual that captures the essence of God's visit to Abram and Sarai is "I've Got a New Name." Just as God changed their name, this may have been the yearnings of our ancestors who unquestionably existed and worked under pseudonyms as chattel. The thought of freedom from those surroundings through death may have prompted for them a better theological understanding of the biblical meaning of Abraham's and Sarah's change; and moreover Jesus' promise of a new name. Think too that as life existed during slavery, a name could be taken away, and a new one doled out, in what was a mere human wholesale property exchange. Yet the earnest hope of a heavenly arrival with a new name which no one could take away may have prompted a gleeful plantation chant such as:

"I've got a new name over in glory,
And it's mine, mine, mine.
I've got a new name over in glory,
And it's mine, mine, mine. [26]

Here emerges some thoughts on the Genesis promise given; from Abram to Abraham, the former name meant High or Exalted Father. However, God's new name for him, Abraham meant "Father of a Multitude. Now with this new name, God meant that each time Abraham would speak his name, "he would be reminded of God's promise" to make him the father of nations."[28] From Sarai to Sarah, his wife named first as a princess, now becomes a noble woman, the bearer of the son who would be the seed for all nations. From this seed that she would bear, not only would "kings of nations" come forth, but also it would be the lineage for the "King of Kings." Interestingly enough neither of them were at an age where this would seem even possible, as Abraham was ninety-nine, and Sarah, ninety years old. But it is indicated that when God changes one's name, it is intended to either signify a change in character, or it is indicative that God is making a major call on the life of that person. The most important change for both Abraham and Sarah was that their new names were unique, since God inserted in each a part of His own name, and since they both were receiving a new and uncharacteristic dignity. Ah! *(Selah!)*

When we arrive "Over in glory" we know that our new names will be like DNA, unlike any other ever given. That is what Jesus promises to any of us who "has an ear to hear" the Holy Spirit, and any who overcomes the world. He promises us a new name which no one else, but we ourselves can know (Revelation 2:17). So yes, then what a joy it will be when we can truly claim "it's mine." Thus with Abraham and Sarah, God's covenant of the new name brought with it the call for them and generations to be firmly purposed to walk with Him by faith. The new name brought with it also the call for them to know by faith that God would do, what God promised he would do! Abraham and Sarah were faithful over-comers! The Hebrews writer affirms their great faith as both are named to the great cloud of witnesses who walked by faith and not by sight.

Baptism is often an end result of the Lenten Season journey. So we find with Baptism by water and the Holy Spirit, we are offered new freedoms in Christ, and thus we earn a new name. We must not only walk with the eyes of faith, but we must trust God as He effects the major changes in our lives. If we conscientiously would work to exercise that same kind of trusting faith such as that of Abraham and Sarah on our earthly walk, God will honor our faithfulness, and we too can count on the promise of that new name over in glory! And I know that I for one will be so glad to sing "And it's mine, mine, mine!" How about you?

ಬಂಎ

Reference:

"As slaves, African Americans weren't allowed to name their children; the slave owners did that. Sometimes they received new names on the ships that brought them from Africa. However, parents named their children in secret, and in their own communities they were known by the names their parents had given them. It wasn't until after the Civil War that African Americans were allowed to name their children, and they began using names that had, until then, been prohibited. They also created names, looking to their African roots for inspiration; this practice became very common in the 1960s, and it helped establish a firm African American identity."
Source:
http://wiki.name.com/en/All_About_Names

ಬಂಎ

Wednesday— after the 2nd Sunday in Lent   Reading: Genesis 17:1-7, 15-16

Your Study Notes Regarding Patriarchal Promises

Do you know what your name means? Make an online or book search to see what you might find. Does your name tell anything that you yourself or others have observed about your life?

_____

_____

_____

_____

_____

_____

_____

_____

_____

_____

_____

_____

_____

_____

_____

_____

Thursday –after the 2ⁿᵈ Sunday in Lent   **Reading: John 21: 18-25**

A Positive Proclamation

Let the church say: "Be Solemnly Assured!"

It is with the "Amen!" that we close prayers not only spoken but also some that are sung. There are many theologians who consider, and with much supportive evidence, a song to be a prayer. From the oldest of traditions, at the end of a prayer, Amen has been used to confirm "so it is," "so be it," or "may it be fulfilled." The 15ᵗʰ century church reformer Martin Luther wrote in advice to his barber, that "you must always speak the Amen firmly. Never doubt that God in His mercy will surely hear you and say yes to your prayers." [29] In other words be solemnly assured.

Furthermore we find when the whole of an assembly responds to prayer with "Amen," it represents each person's acceptance of the spoken words as his own, and confirms that which has been said as true. Sometimes even in common conversations, it is often evident that individual statements of certainty also are concluded or ratified with "Amen." From the Hebrew into Greek into Latin and into English the word "Amen" is still the same, a universal word. It is one of the best known words among human language. Moreover, Amen in biblical language is also used to begin conversations too.

Jesus spoke the "Amen" many times as he began a conversation to signify that his listeners could be solemnly assured it was truth. His words might have been in the form of what we read in our particular translations of the Bible as "Verily...," "Most assuredly..." or "Truly..."

Nonetheless, His point was that one could be absolutely sure, solemnly assured of what was said. There was no need for further question. Here consider some of the declarations that would follow Jesus' absolute assurance; we find him sharing truths like:

Truly I say to you, whatever you shall bind on earth shall be bound in heaven; and whatever you loose on earth shall be loosed in heaven. *(Matthew18:18)* or,

Verily I say unto you, whosoever shall not receive the kingdom of God as a little child, he shall not enter therein. *(Mark 10:17)* or,

"**Truly**, I say to you, among those born of women there has not arisen anyone greater than John the Baptist; yet he who is least in the kingdom of heaven is greater than he. *(Matthew 11:11)* or,

Jesus answered and said to him, "**Most assuredly**, I say to you, unless one is born again, he cannot see the kingdom of God." *(John 3:3)* or,

And He said to him, "**Truly** I say to you, today you shall be with Me in Paradise."*(Luke 23:43)*

With this new or even an improved understanding of Jesus' solemn assurances and the "Amen," let us each join in sharing some absolute Bible truth with somebody today. And when again we find ourselves amidst the congregation taking part genuinely in prayer or song, each of us now may be compelled to agree, and will speak more firmly when the Church says: *AMEN!*[30]

Thursday –after the 2ⁿᵈ Sunday in Lent   **Reading: John 21: 18-25**

Your Study Notes Regarding Positive Proclamations

Describe how you use the word Amen most often. Search today's scripture reading and list the Positive proclamations. What is the emphasized truth that John offers in verses 24 and 25?

_____

_____

_____

_____

_____

_____

_____

_____

_____

_____

_____

_____

_____

_____

_____

_____

_____

_____

Friday—after the 2ⁿᵈ Sunday in Lent   **Reading: Luke 7: 11-23**

Procession of Pity

"When the Lord saw her, He had compassion on her and said to her, "Do not weep." –Luke 7:13 NKJRV

When I was a very young girl, I often had to go with my grand-parents to the funerals of their extended family and friends. I can remember quite vividly, the weighted sorrow that swept over many of those bereaved families. I remember the long line of cars with the headlights shining as the funeral procession moved from the church to what then was typically called the graveyard. The days that I remember could have ranged anywhere from an overcast, clouded and misty day to one in which the setting of the evening sun blanketed the sky in deep red to purple colors as a fitting welcome to the dearly departed. The sense of an inconsolable widow now left alone, or a husband or children tearing with painful grief was so surreal for me as a child. Then the evening following at home really would seem so somber. And on one of these days, as my Granddaddy went about his evening chores or just sat in front of the fireplace, I can remember him just humming softly one or two hymns, particularly *"Shall We Meet Beyond the River"*[31] and *"Come Ye Disconsolate."*[32] You see I never heard him sing much at all, but at these times, I would imagine he inwardly felt the comfort of these songs; he probably knew that one day he would see the beloved one or dear friend again and for sure at this moment earth had *"no sorrow that Heaven cannot heal."*

Lazarus, a close friend, was dead. Jesus felt great sorrow for His sisters, Mary and Martha. This is the human quality of peculiar interest that the gospel writers were sure to capture about their Master. How He had compassion for those around Him was a story of peculiarity perhaps to them but certainly worth retelling. There is the note on how he wept upon the news of Lazarus' death. There is the note of how he wept when he rode into Jerusalem and viewed a city that was essentially clueless. Thoughtfulness, gentleness, and great compassion were characteristics of our Loving Lord and Savior.

Well before Lazarus' death, passing by the gate to the city of Nain, as a funeral crowd was headed out, and observing all so quickly, Jesus being emotionally stirred touched the bier of the son of a widow. Touching it meant that those bearing the body should stop. With all eyes turned to Him, a stranger, who would stop this procession, its probably imaginative that you could hear the sweeping sudden hush of the mourners. His audible and tender urging to this mother, "Do not weep" brings her literally in this moment before the mercy seat of God. With the greatest of compassion for this mother, he commands the young dead man to arise. Here Jesus offers the despaired mother the kind of comfort only heaven could heal. There is now joy where the heart was desolate and wounded. For the young man, new life is now a reality, and his miraculous resuscitation a phenomenon— since it was certainly enough of a crowd to confirm he was truly dead. This ranked as one of those reports Jesus wanted John's disciples to carry back. He had raised the dead and because of His divine yet human compassion He would do it again. At some time later, His loving words to Lazarus' sisters would in effect say, "Oh Mary Don't You Weep; tell Martha not to mourn;" come to the Mercy Seat! His words to His own earthly mother would be expressions of tender love for her care as He himself embraced death on the cross, even as He knew there would be resurrection.

Thinking back on those times as a child when the families I saw stood before the graves with wounded hearts, makes me wonder what did they believe then about resurrection? Did they know there would be new life for their loved one again? Did they resolve eventually to wait for the comfort of Jesus tenderly saying, "Earth has no sorrow that heaven cannot heal?" I can now think my Granddaddy believed and was comforted during those times.

As with the story of the son and mother of Nain, no matter how dire the situation, we can be reminded that Jesus in his God-Man compassion offers us joy, light, and hope. As He gave Martha an absolute truth in saying, "I am the resurrection and the life," we too should respond, "Yes Lord, I believe." Yes, we should come to him if we are dejected, depressed, sorrowful or sad. We should come to the "Mercy Seat, fervently kneeling" thinking on Jesus' tenderness when He from the cross consoles His own mother: "Behold your Son." Or we could ponder His promise that: "I have come so that they may have life, and that they may have it more abundantly." We too will come away from such an encounter rejoicing and glorifying God, just as the widow and people of Nain. We too will come away knowing "Earth has no sorrow that heaven cannot cure."

Friday—after the 2nd Sunday in Lent   **Reading: Luke 7: 11-23**

Your Study Notes Regarding Pity

In what ways have you seen deep compassion shown to people you know or have observed from a distance?

_____

_____

_____

_____

_____

_____

_____

_____

_____

_____

_____

_____

_____

_____

_____

_____

_____

_____

_____

_____

Providential Care

"Give us this day, our daily bread, you said you would
Supply all our needs, according to your riches,
I have but to ask and I will receive." —Edwin Hawkins

An interesting thought occurs on contemplating Jesus' reply to Satan's suggestion that He turn the stones into bread. "Man shall not live by bread alone but by every word that is spoken out of the mouth of God." Just think about it, in the beginning God spoke the worlds into creation and He said, "That's good!" Then God spoke, "Let us make man in our image, after our likeness." Man could not come into existence without the spoken word of God.

Is there a double-edged implication here that Jesus references? Man in his spiritual state, cannot exist or survive by just food alone. Yet in his physical state, man needs not only physical bread, but also God's Word just to wake up each day. We know that all God speaks is good! His perfect instruction and His providential care, right down to the daily bread, is the way he still speaks forth our daily re-creation in a spiritual and physical way. Just as the sun rises and runs its circuit day-to-day, so each of us individually are graced to rise and set, with an opportunity to burst forth each new day after having rested in our natural and silent state. Therefore our sheer subsistence depends upon the blessing of God speaking forth our continuation each day. We are kept by the every word that comes from the mouth of God. Kurt Carr puts it this way, "I almost let go *[temptation]*, but God kept me *[grace]*."[33]

Daily we need God's perfect instruction to find our way through the wilderness experiences of this world and to avert the snares of temptation such as Jesus experienced. During the exodus from Egypt and forty years of wilderness wanderings, the Israelites experienced the providential care of God. His guiding presence was a pillar of cloud by day, and a pillar of fire by night to lead, and help them find their way. He spoke the words, and bread from heaven, manna [Hebrew: *what is this*] it was called, fell every day and every one gathered it according to their needs. The Holy Spirit was God's guiding presence for Jesus during His forty days in the wilderness. But unlike the Israelites, Jesus withstood the temptations without complaint! He suffered but still He accomplished the perfect will of God!

We too like Jesus, can be led by God's guiding presence during these remaining days of Lent through devout fasting and praying. In doing so, we are thus positioned to ask that the words we speak and our heartfelt meditations be acceptable to His will, meriting us daily re-creation!

Not only daily bread, but Lord we need your spoken words of love, peace, joy, *This Day.*"[34]

Saturday—after the 2nd Sunday in Lent   **Reading: Psalm 19**

Your Study Notes Regarding God's Providential Care

Write down a petition to God for one thing that you really would desire that He re-create in your life according to His will. Earnestly pray your petition written here daily until he speaks forth the fulfillment of your desire. Be sure to make a note when you see the fulfillment of the time in days (or hours/minutes/years).

_____

_____

_____

_____

_____

_____

_____

_____

_____

_____

_____

_____

_____

_____

_____

_____

_____

_____

Sunday- Third Sunday in Lent   **Reading: Genesis 9:8-17**

Unconditional Promises

The sign of the first covenant that God (Yahweh) ever established was the rainbow. It was the "outward and visible reminder" of His promise to mankind.[35] Every time we see a rainbow, we should be reminded that God remembers! What He remembers is His everlasting and unconditional guarantee to bond with mankind.

Likewise the bread and the wine are signs, in some sense of thinking, of the "last covenant." These tangible symbols, Jesus explained to His Disciples during the Last Supper, are to be the spiritual guarantee of unending salvation for all believers. They symbolize the sacrifice of "My body and My blood" for the forgiveness of all sin.

Reflect on this thought today or as often as we celebrate the communion. With the breaking of the bread we are charged to remember how brutally the body of our crucified Savior was broken ("Do this in remembrance of me"). As we take the cup and drink the wine, we remember that every drop of Jesus' blood formed the seal on this "last" and New Covenant for the eternal cleansing of all sin! The seal of a high authority or a seal embossed on paper -notarized, always implies "this thing is true". We must remember then, that the blood of Christ is the seal and authentic imprint for eternity. Jesus offers an authentic testimony of Himself as He spoke "I am the Truth!"—that is an absolute and unconditional promise.

At its sighting, a rainbow is still an awesome scene at which to gaze. The brilliance of the colors in the midst of blue skies should grab our attention as a reminder of God's promise. In our celebration of the communion there is also an awesome reminder. It is "the bread and the wine" we take; and if we consent to it, these symbols still serve to revive our commitment and union with Christ Jesus.

So today, we should sing with joy a song of remembrance at the Lord's Table in celebration of God's unconditional promises for each of us. It could be a song such as— *"We Remember You."* [36]

"As we drink this cup, we worship you;
As we eat this bread, we honor you;
And we offer You our lives as You have offered Yours for us.
We remember all You've done for us,
We remember Your covenant with us,
We remember, and worship You, O Lord."

Sunday- Third Sunday in Lent   **Reading: Genesis 9:8-17**

Your Study Notes Regarding Unconditional Promises

Under what circumstances would you be able to make an unconditional promise to someone? Make notes based on today's reading about God's promises.

_____

_____

_____

_____

_____

_____

_____

_____

_____

_____

ℰↄℭℛ

Fact: Yahweh in Hebrew means "Covenant God." Yahweh, this God of Covenant is mentioned in every chapter of Book IV of the Psalms (90-106).

Encouragement: Turn to Psalm 103 and sing "Bless Yahweh, O my Soul! And all that is within me, bless His holy name!"

ℰↄ ℭℛ

Monday after the Third Sunday   **Reading: Luke 13: 1-17**

Parables and Perishing Points

"The Lord is not willing that any should perish, but that all should come to repentance" –2 Peter 3:9

Repent or perish! Bear fruit or be cut down! Purge righteous hypocrisy! These were three perishing points that Jesus tried to explain to his hearers and those synagogue rulers. Living today in a society where animals can get lavish treatment while people starve to death, it may be easy to identify with Jesus' rebuke to purge the righteous hypocrisy.

I heard Dr. David Jeremiah once preach that "Parables change the way people think about the kingdom of God." Jesus spoke in parables so that His Hearers could easily interpret the "point", and maybe change their way of thinking. In Luke's record (13:1-9) of His comments and furthermore His parable about the fig tree, the point should have been quite clear. Israel would be given one more chance to get their act together, which says, one more chance to repent; otherwise, they would perish, similarly like the Galileans did at the hands of Pilate. In the parable following, the keeper of the vineyard would rescue the non-productive fig tree. Likewise, Jesus would save those whom God the Father in his wrath would cut down for lack of bearing life-yielding fruit.

In our modern society for some, there's an acceptable standard to over-indulge for the care of pets and many other material possessions; yet from perhaps a cross section of the same populace, there could be meager commitment to care for human lives crippled by the evil spirit of poverty. At the same time our society through channels of mass media, often promotes the blame-game of sins being worse for some than for others. Moreover, many are quick to issue the guilty verdicts rather than intercede with compassion in offering the perishing a second chance.

John Wesley so rightly says "Your approbation now outweighs your prejudices." [37]

So what will change the minds of a society? As Bishop R.L. Speaks suggested, "Only the power of the Holy Spirit can *change* and purify our corrupt self and our corrupt society."[38] Jesus put the ruler of the synagogue and His adversaries to shame as He reminded them of a perishing point of their own hypocrisy: On the Sabbath even they loosed the animals that were tied up for watering; should not one of their own sisters in the line of Abraham, bound by a "Spirit of infirmity" for so long be loosed on the Sabbath? Should there not be a passion for God to do His own work on His own Sabbath, rather than some more convenient day?

Fanny J. Crosby described in a well-known hymn words that remind us of what Jesus is saying:

"Rescue the perishing, care for the dying,
Snatch them in pity from sin and the grave,
weep o'er the erring one, Lift up the fallen,
Tell them of Jesus the mighty to save."

Just as He lifted up and loosed the woman bowed in her infirmity, Jesus too can lift us who with "unsanctified hearts are under this spirit of infirmity."[39] Let us pray today that we may understand better His parables and the perishing points of His Word.

Prayer: Merciful God, through the anointing of your Holy Spirit help us to see and act upon the pressing demands of right now in our lives. Let us be ever mindful of your righteous forgiveness in our lives and always repentant in our hearts; help us daily to turn, turn away from those things that can so easily corrupt and distract us, and turn to you the Author and Finisher of our faith. In the name of Jesus we pray, Amen.

Monday after the Third Sunday   **Reading: Luke 13: 1-17**

Your Study Notes on Parables and Perishing Points

Find two other of Jesus' parables you may have read before and did not understand. Re-read them today and make notes here.

_____

_____

_____

_____

_____

_____

_____

_____

_____

_____

_____

_____

_____

_____

_____

_____

_____

_____

_____

Tuesday –after the 3ʳᵈ Sunday in Lent   **Reading: Exodus 20:1-17**

God's Preamble to the Promise – "I am the Lord Your God"

"The law was not given as a means of salvation. It was given to a people already saved in order to instruct them in the will of the Lord so that they might fulfill God's purpose for them as "a kingdom of priests and a holy nation". The revelation was given not to give but to guide life." -Wycliffe's Commentary[40]

A friend of mine often say's that the simplest law of life we daily can observe is that of the traffic light law. It guides how traffic moves in an orderly manner. Red says we need to stop. Green says we need to go. Yellow offers us the opportunity to exercise caution. Tragic accidents occur often when the rule of orderly movement is disobeyed. So it is often when the laws of life are defied, catastrophic mishaps may be the sole consequence.

In the giving of the Law, God offered the Israelites a way to avoid the mishaps of disorder along their journey away from Egypt. In obeying the law, God offered them the option to cultivate a closer relationship with Him –think on this as worship. They also would be required to nurture the relationships with those who were within their community—this would be life. He emphasized upfront, I am your God, who delivered you, my people. Despite the gift of the law, they wandered in the desert long enough for a generation to die out because of their inherent defiance. It was their disobedience to the law that often brought about calamitous effects along the Exodus trail.

Thousands of years later, it is important to observe that Jesus in his masterful teaching held the Exodus laws governing life and worship in high esteem. In response to the Pharisee who questioned "what is the greatest commandment?", He summed up the duty each person had in the manner of loving God first with everything that one had, and loving one's neighbor as one would love himself. Jesus assured them all other laws, God given, and those created by man-made, were predicated upon these two. Another way he taught the law as divine guidance was to simply say that "whatever you want men to do to you, do also to them" for this is the Law and the Prophets. Contrast Moses as being the priestly go-between to ensure that the people kept the agreement and law in fulfilling God's will for worship and their lives. Compare Jesus as being the priestly Messiah serving as the fulfillment of God's will for total communion.

In these modern times there are still consequences to rebelling against God's divine order. With our disobedience of the law, often we still can see and even sometimes experience devastating and catastrophic consequences—broken fellowships, broken relationships, broken homes, and broken lives. Journeying through our Sinai deserts of this present age, we are admonished in our hymn singing to "Trust and Obey, for there is no other way." [41]

The simple laws of red-light, green-light are in a sense symbolic of the all encompassing logic God grants us through his grace and mercy. Moreover, unlike the Israelites, we are not a saved people. Individually we must seek the kingdom and accept salvation in order to align our lives in obedience to Kingdom purposes and God's Holiness. We must also strive to trust God in our wilderness wanderings, as well as obey Him. So in the words sung to the A.M.E. church's closing response to all of the Decalogue, let us continually pray: "Lord, have mercy upon us, and write these laws upon our hearts."

ℰℐℭℛ

The Decalogue, from the Greek translation meaning "ten words" or, in Hebrew, (Ex 34:28; Deut 4:13; 10:4), is more commonly known as the Ten Commandments.

This material is first encountered in Exodus 20, but the number ten and the familiar two-tablet description initially occur in Exodus 34. The Decalogue sits at the center of the covenant between God and Israel, as mediated through Moses.

Source: http://www.ivpress.com/title/exc/1781-X.pdf

ℰℐℭℛ

Tuesday –after the 3rd Sunday in Lent   **Reading: Exodus 20:1-17**

Your Study Notes Regarding God's Preamble

How do you see the first two commandments as the foundation for the Ten Commandments?

_____

_____

_____

_____

_____

_____

_____

_____

_____

_____

_____

_____

_____

_____

_____

_____

_____

_____

Wednesday—after the 3rd Sunday in Lent   **Reading: John 2:13-22**

Purging the Pollution

—I Love thy church, O God! Her walls before thee stand dear as the apple of thine eye, and graven on thy Hand. —Timothy Dwight [42]

— "Then, going over to the people who sold doves, he told them, "Get these things out of here. Don't turn my Father's house into a marketplace!" —John 2:16-The Message

The Matthew Henry commentary suggests that our "hearts and lives are to be purged similarly" as Jesus threw all of those corrupted moneychangers out of the temple courts. First He drove them all out —drove their cattle with a whip, threw out their dirty money behind them, and then turned over their tables to show they would never again be welcomed to make His Father's house a den of thieves. What Love! Jesus loved the temple of God. As a twelve year-old child he sat in this place impressing and counseling the old folks with His wisdom and knowledge, being about His Father's business! He rebuked His earthly parents concern for his disappearance with an authoritative "where else would you expect that I would be" kind of response? Furthermore, in many New Testament passages, you find reference to Jesus being in the temple. During his younger years he was a Son in His Father's House. During His public ministry He was faithful as a Son over God's house. (Hebrews 3:6)

You see in the temple, there is the Glory of God! Nothing should be allowed to corrupt His Holy place. You find up on the mountain, even the sandals that Moses wore, had to be removed because of the Holiness of God's presence there. You will find in the temple there also is Salvation. If that which occupies the sanctuary of God is corrupt, how can the radiance and saving grace of God's presence abide? Even the secular historian Josephus recorded how God's light did not emanate from the temple for 200 years because of His displeasure with the "transgressions of His laws." [43]

Now at this point, Jesus knew the high priests and the Sadducees sanctioned what went on in the temple, but on this day, he just got fed up. The moneychangers were defiling the Holiness of the physical temple; they were transgressing the Law. Jesus' mission was to expose their corrupt and deficient faith.

Understand further that it seems great corruptions increase in the church likewise in our times as well due to the love of money. Many in our contemporary culture show a great disrespect for the temple of God. The love of the church that the hymnist describes is a holy value inevitably crowded out by the programs designed to meet the conveniences of the people. The true and spiritual worship of God ranks secondary in many of these type sanctuaries. Thus the holiness of the worship space is often tarnished. It's not unusual to find some people who line up to hawk merchandise in the "physical sanctuaries" similarly as the moneychangers did. The streams of news headlines reporting misuse, abuse, mismanagement, and litigations against clergy and lay people demonstrate another subtle yet broader means of contempt for the sanctity of the church as a whole.

Jesus' avowal that the church is a "House of Prayer" rather than a den of thieves still applies. As present day pilgrims, prayer should stand as the "sweet communion" that draws us into deeper love for the church and "her heavenly ways." Pray today for the Holy temples of America.

Paul also tells us in I Corinthians 6:19, that our bodies are a holy temple sanctified to the Glory of God. What then shall we do with our heart and our life if we allow it to be contaminated with the refuse of the world? The Jewish pilgrims became comfortable with the conveniences the money changers offered. We too can become at ease allowing the worldly rubbish to penetrate our "inner courts." Today let's ask the Holy Spirit for a purging of our individual and corporate temples to make more room for God's glory. Just like Jesus, let us take on a deeper fervor, a deeper passion, and love for the church—the place where God's holiness abides. Let this mind be in us that was also in Christ Jesus to just purge the pollution! Amen!

Wednesday—after the 3rd Sunday in Lent   **Reading: John 2:13-22**

Your Study Notes Regarding Purging Pollution

Think about the things in your life that need purging? What can you do to effect the purge process?

_____

_____

_____

_____

_____

_____

_____

_____

_____

_____

_____

_____

_____

_____

_____

_____

_____

_____

Thursday—after the 3ʳᵈ Sunday in Lent   **Reading: John 5:1-18**

Paralyzed by the Pool

"Sittin' around waitin' to die" is a phraseology that one of my friends uses to describe what some of his older and retired lifetime acquaintances do daily. This he describes as their inability to see that there is still life to be lived. They would rather just sit at home with the complaints of de-habilitating illnesses rather than strive to get up and do things for life. How often do we encounter such people in our families or social circles? These people who look for sympathy from others? It reminds me of the story of the day that Jesus went to the spa!

Surely His stopping there was not a happenstance visit that day. Everything Jesus did was intentional. In some translations of the story we find the pool of Bethesda is beside the Sheep Gate in Jerusalem. It was a pool that housed five porches, and that purportedly bubbled. The Hebrew rendering of *beth eshda* defines it as a "Place of Outpouring, or a House of Grace. The pool of Bethesda then was the site where the sick and afflicted would wait yearly for the Angel of the Lord to come and trouble or stir-up the water for healing; they waited for the outpouring of God's grace.

I can just imagine the presence of my Lord Jesus as he enters this healing spa on the Sabbath. He entered with the intent to find just one man! Surely he knew exactly where he would be; particularly since the man had been lying here for thirty-eight years, "waitin' to die" in essence, as there was no one at hand to put him in the water. Or as he further explained to Jesus, others would step in before him. This man had the desire for healing, as he still stayed here in this place, but lacked the means for his own healing to be realized. It is interesting that Jesus does not even address his comments as there are none noted in John's accounting of the scene.

This leads me to believe that Jesus really doesn't want to hear our excuses. He just wants us to answer the pertinent question, just as he wanted this man to answer: "Do you want to be made well?" And why does Jesus ask the question? So that he can immediately pour out His Grace and Mercy upon us, just as he did for this paralyzed man!

Are we ever paralyzed with fear of not being able to move further from where we are in life? Would we prefer to stay on the porches with the masses of sick and afflicted in this world waiting for a miracle, or would we prefer to look to Jesus in faith, with a trusting heart, and live, rising up from where we are so paralyzed?

Rather than immersing him in the water of this pool at Bethesda, Jesus immediately immerses this man in the living water! Just speaking the Word, Jesus saturates him with the water which springs from the fountain of everlasting life! This man was flooded by the supernatural healing of the Almighty God. He only needed to do as Jesus commanded him now: "Rise, take up your bed, and walk!"

The means of healing had been realized, and surely this poor soul must have been astonished beyond measure as he obeyed the command without any hesitation. He didn't need anyone to assist him with this healing process; with Jesus' strength imparted to him, he could carry his bed for himself. When he was questioned about carrying his bed on the Sabbath, probably still in a euphoric and joyous state, he could only reply, "He who made me well *told* me to take up my bed and walk!" And that was all he knew! What more do we need to know if Jesus speaks to the heart of our desires? Nothing more than to obey! Do that what He tells us to do! Indeed it is important to know that before John ends this story, it is with intent stated what the consequences of not following Jesus' counsel would be. You see Jesus Himself catches up with the man again in a supernatural way, and warns him not to sin any more, "lest a worse thing come upon you."

The warning is still prevalent as God's Word is the same yesterday, today and forever. Jesus still admonishes us to know that we cannot take God's healing forgiveness, grace or mercy lightly. It is strength given to us to move us from where we are stuck in life, but more importantly it is given for His Glory! *(Selah!)*

Prayer: I praise you God for the revelation of your living word this day. Let it dwell in my heart eternally. Help me to trust more each day Jesus' commands for healing in my life! Help me to encourage others who sit and wait helplessly, to know there is hope for continued life, here in the present, the future, and eternally. Amen.

Thursday—after the 3rd Sunday in Lent　　　　Reading: John 5:1-18

Your Study Notes Regarding Paralyzed by the Pool

In what ways do you know that fear of something has kept you para-lyzed for a period of time? Re-read the scripture and make notes to compare with how you moved on, or how you plan to move away from fearfulness.

_____

_____

_____

_____

_____

_____

_____

_____

_____

_____

_____

_____

_____

_____

_____

_____

_____

_____

Friday–after the 3rd Sunday in Lent   **Reading: 1 Cor. 10: 1-13**

Priceless!—Liquid Prayers

How priceless is your unfailing love, O God!
People take refuge in the shadow of your wings. Psalms 31: 7

The question was asked: Besides the death of Lazarus, at what other time did Jesus cry?

In addition to the time when Jesus wept outside the tomb of his friend Lazarus (John 11.35), Jesus "wept over" the city of Jerusalem on the day we call Palm Sunday (Luke 19.41-42). Four days later in the Garden of Gethsemane, in great "anguish" his "sweat became like great drops of blood falling down on the ground" (Luke 22.43-44). This was not exactly weeping, but similar in that Jesus was praying intensely as He was in agony. It was out of an unfailing love that Jesus wept for Lazarus and Jerusalem. He wanted to protect both. It was out of an unfailing love that He knew He would have to drink the cup at Calvary.

Why is Jesus weeping? The scriptures tell us He was one filled with much compassion. Jesus wanted to place Jerusalem under his wing because He saw they were blinded to the true nature of His kingdom, and the acclaim he received. While riding on a donkey through the city, just as it was prophesied of a Messiah, this acclaim would be short-lived. So with a heavy heart, as he is drawing near, he weeps from the burden of a people who could not recognize all that God had done, even from the exodus of Egypt to the return from exile in Babylon. Jerusalem at this point does not want to take refuge in his Messianic authority.

He sees this as he approaches the temple to find the moneychangers and other merchants being fraudulent to the people, to the poor mostly. He fulfills His authority with respect to cleansing the temple of these "thieves" who would commercialize and dishonestly use the sacrificial system established by God, His Father. Here He is really angry! He professes already to the hardened hearts of the Pharisees and rulers: "He who sees Me see Him who sent Me"

Matthew Henry's Commentary sums it up as such: "The Son of God did not weep, *vain and causeless* tears, nor for a light matter, nor for himself. *He knows the value of souls*, [He knows] the weight of guilt, and how low it will press and sink mankind. May he then come and cleanse our hearts by his Spirit, from all that defiles."

We may find ourselves in situations that will cause us to cry. Crying is not only cleansing, but also a delicate method of entreating God for a cause. Sometimes the burdens we carry cause us to weep out of despair. But God reminds us that He will not put any more on us than we can bear. We must remember too that Jesus has experienced the ultimate of emotions that we too feel. Yet His tears were tears of unfailing love.

Prayer: Lord Jesus, on every side, help us to become attentive to the words of your truth and salvation. Help us to pray intensely with compassion for those who cannot see your unfailing love in their lives. Teach us to value more each day the price of your unfailing love for us. Amen.

Friday–after the 3rd Sunday in Lent   *Reading: 1 Cor. 10: 1-13*

Your Study Notes Regarding Priceless—Liquid Prayers

How has God ministered his unfailing love in your life at times of weeping?

Saturday—after the 3rd Sunday in Lent   **Reading Psalm 107:1-3, 17-22**

My Praise

"How can I say thanks for the things you have done for me, things so underserved, yet you gave to prove your love for me. The voices of a million angels could not express my gratitude, all that I am and ever hope to be; I owe it all to you. To God be the Glory, To God be the Glory, to God be the Glory, for the things he has done..."— "My Tribute" by Andrae Crouch

Andrae Crouch's hymn of praise to God for all He has done, offers us a profound prayer of praise. Praising God for His Goodness and Mercy is an essential prayer we Christians daily should exercise. In the bible, God's steadfast love is often translated from the Hebrew word "*Hesed*", meaning mercy. His Mercy is often paired in the Psalms with the word for his Goodness, rendered in Hebrew as *dox*. This root word *dox* gives us an understanding of why we could consider this hymn, "My Tribute" a doxology. It offers up praise to God's glory for His goodness and His mercy.

Then as a spiritual insight from Psalm 23, we find that His Goodness and Mercy are paired to pursue each of us for the rest of our lives. Dr. Frank B. Meyer personifies these "blessed attributes" of Goodness and Mercy as our "Celestial Escorts, twin Angels of God". He says, "Not Goodness alone, for we are sinners needing forgiveness. Not Mercy alone, for we need many things besides forgiveness."[44] So we can understand better perhaps that all of the days of our lives we are blessed; we are blessed in health, in sickness, and in dying with the following of "the rear guard" of and the pursuit of God's steadfast love and His Goodness. Time and again in the sickness of our physical bodies, and in the sickness of our spiritual bodies, God's Goodness and Mercy restores our soul! Who would not rejoice in praise for this kind of deliverance?

Envision a sick and dying world. See God's mercy as the stream that flows from the fountain of His goodness. See the sick and dying as thirsty pilgrims in the desert such as the Israelites were during their exodus from Egypt. See the water streaming from the Rock of ages. Observe that Jesus Himself declares in the midst of the Feast of the Tabernacle that He right now is the symbol and fulfillment of that flowing stream. He right now is Goodness and Mercy in the flesh—the fountain and the stream! Here He invites all who are thirsty to come to Him (John 7:37).

Thirsty could very well translate as sin-sick and weary, impoverished or penniless. It is necessary however to understand the customary ritual at this festival was the filling of a golden pitcher which would be carried from the pool of Siloam each day to the temple. The ritual reminded Israel of the water that streamed from the rock in the desert (Num. 20:2-13). On this occasion, some have speculated that Jesus perhaps stood, interrupting this ritual as the water was being poured out of the pitcher. Forget the pool of Siloam! Forget the pool of Bethesda. Here he stood, offering a deep well, a rich well, and a free well from which whosoever—all could draw. Be reminded on the other hand too that this disruption ultimately was one more event that led to the Jews wanting His arrest and crucifixion.

In looking toward Easter, we all have such glorious reasons to give thanks for a dying and resurrected Savior who indeed is Goodness and Mercy. It is because with His blood, He has saved us— he has redeemed us! Therefore let the redeemed thank God for His Goodness and His Mercy. With His power, just as He is resurrected, He too has raised us! Therefore let the redeemed thank God for His Goodness and His Mercy!

If we are spiritually thirsty, let us not be slow to realize that we indeed have a fountain from which we can drink freely. And if we have drunk this holy water and abound in the depths of God's Goodness and Mercy, let us rejoice in praise with the redeemed. So for today's suggested meditative work out: Thank God for His Goodness and Mercy while singing "To God Be the Glory, for the things He has done!" Amen!!

Saturday—after the 3rd Sunday in Lent   **Reading Psalm 107:1-3, 17-22**

Your Study Notes Regarding My Praise

Read also the Numbers 20:1-13 scripture today. Describe the goodness and mercy God offered the children of Israel. How are you thankful today?

_____

_____

_____

_____

_____

_____

_____

_____

_____

_____

_____

_____

_____

_____

_____

_____

_____

Fourth Sunday in Lent   **Reading: Luke 15:1-3, 11b-32**

Politics and Protocols?

In 1748 and subsequent years, John Newton personally experienced the absolute wonder of a merciful God. The astonishing act of mercy on God's part for him led him to write words that would be put to music such as "Amazing grace, how sweet the sound, that saved a wretch like me." Perhaps it could be viewed that in his own self-righteousness, as a young man Newton felt his pedigree was much better than those persons he trafficked through the Middle Passage. You see John Newton was a slave trader, and slave ship captain, an unconscionable work. It even took Newton some thirty-four years later after admitted conversion and leaving the slave trade, while yet all that time being a preacher in England, to actually confess how wrong being a part of the slave trade had been. He at that point became convicted of his wrongs and labored as an advocate against slavery. But at an old age suffering from bouts of memory loss, he confessed what he still remembered was "I am a great sinner and that Christ is a great Savior." It is through the mercy of God, this one sinner's life was so dramatically changed. [45] Generations later people experience joy over this one sinner's written testimony of amazing forgiveness and grace –"how sweet the sound."

So if we turn to the story Luke offers about sinners, can you imagine how flabbergasted the Pharisees and Scribes were when Jesus sat to eat with sinners and tax collectors? How dare He? This sect felt they themselves were the righteous, over-achievers in their community; they had pedigree. How dare He dine with them and then afterward entertain the low-life of their community? The tax collectors were detested because of their deceptive tactics for extorting the taxes, which might similarly compare nowadays to how some pawn dealers extract their interest on loans. But speaking of deception, these same rulers would invite Jesus to eat bread with them and although camouflaged in self-righteousness, they really had a hidden agenda. It would provide them an opportunity to further condemn Jesus. Have you ever sat in a meeting among folks who you felt had hidden agendas? *(Hold that thought!)*

The rulers of Israel were rather incensed with Jesus by the time they found him headed to Matthew's house. If He was to be a Rabbi, and teacher of the Law, according to their political posture, then He was not keeping protocol according the law. Their righteous indignation now made them complaining accusers. But Jesus deflected their righteous anger with a play on their own words, simply saying "I have not come to call the righteous, but sinners, to repentance." Similarly, he told these rulers "...there will be more joy in heaven over one sinner who repents than over ninety-nine just persons who need no repentance. Jesus knew they suffered from a superiority complex due to their legalistic views. They felt any who did not hold the laws in the strictness of observance as they did were more or less, sinners. They felt they were a whole people! But Jesus' message, following their criticism, set the tone for understanding better why God reaches out for the lost! Penitence is more pleasing to God than political correctness! The things God desires are "a broken heart, and... a contrite spirit" (Psalm 34:18).

So at present days, we still find boardrooms of the self-righteous and politically correct Pharisaic attitudes are in existence. They are often people who are whole and are above the lineage of others! They are as a preacher once said the challengers who "know more about church than they know about God." But Jesus knows now, just as He knew then, that it is the sick that need the Physician. It is the sick that need healing. It is the lost that need to be found. It is a wonder, an amazing wonder to think that God could use a man like John Newton, an infidel who disregarded humanity to become one of the great evangelists of his times in England. It is noted that "genuine repentance brings not only pardon but complete restoration." It is a wonder too that Jesus would say for this is the type that the Shepherd lays on his shoulder, and rejoices because now this lost sheep is found. This lost one is given the best robe of heaven: totally amazing Grace!

Fourth Sunday in Lent   **Reading: Luke 15:1-3, 11b-32**

Politics and Protocols?

Your Study Notes Regarding Politics and Protocols

Make notes on how you think God is no respecter of person.

_____

_____

_____

_____

_____

_____

_____

_____

_____

_____

_____

_____

_____

_____

_____

_____

_____

_____

_____

Monday–after the 4th Sunday in Lent   **Reading: Ephesians 2:1-10**

Power –Past, Present and Projected

"Dead Men Walking" was the title of a book written in the early 1990's by Sister Helen Prejean telling the story of her life's work in New Orleans, Louisiana. The book received wide acclaim and was made into a feature length movie. She was an advocate for the abolition of the death penalty, and spiritual advisor to prisoners who were waiting on Louisiana's Death Row. Due to violent crimes committed in their past, the men she mentored were condemned to death. Her vow was to help them spiritually, and their families, and ultimately the victims' families, during this continuing but concluding process. Her powerful witness of what God could do for these men made their past so unequal to what their present state was during her ministry to them as they faced the ultimate fate of death by electrocution. It was indicated that "Loveless lives" were offered the powerful love of God.

Sister Prejean's desire was to show each of these persons that they could have a partnership with Christ right where they were, although they were condemned by a flawed system. A theme that ran through Sister Prejean's story was one of the "Redemptive Power of Love."

To the Ephesians church, the Apostle Paul described how in their human condition, before knowing the power of Christ Jesus and His resurrection, they were very much like dead men walking: condemned to die eternally. However that was in the past! Now as believers in Christ and His resurrection, life for that deadly human condition to them is presently restored. "Therefore there is no condemnation to those who are in Christ Jesus" (Romans 8:1). The message remains the same for us today. There is no ultimate fate of eternal death if we are in Christ. We who believe <u>are</u> alive with Christ, and resurrected with Christ, and moreover, sit with Christ in heavenly places. This is all due to the manifest grace of our Loving Father, God! His Grace is ever sufficient that we can enjoy all of this power right now through faith.

A recording from the Brooklyn Tabernacle Choir features a refrain from a well known hymn of pardon that sums up this all-sufficient Grace for our present, and for the riches God has in store for us in the future. It is a powerfully sung reprise that simply states:

"Grace, grace, God's grace—grace that will pardon and cleanse within;
Grace, grace, God's grace—grace that is greater than all our sin." [46]

God's grace truly offers us right now the redemptive power of His love. God's grace will take us onward as we are new creations, created in Christ Jesus to do God's work. Greater than anything we have ever had or lacked in our lives previously, we now have the gift of a prepared path of love to travel forward. No condemnation, no biased systems to punish unfairly, or arbitrary claims of injustice are included in God's heavenly order. Do recognize these things such as condemnation, bias, and unfairness still exist however in the "worldly order." But let us praise God today for creating order out of disorder, for making lives that had no "rhyme or reason", lives of balance. All of this we find as Christ's redemptive love moves us to a higher level of faith, away from the worldly systems. And more importantly, let us thank God for overpowering condemnation, and projecting for each of us the liberty and freedom of future and eternal fellowship. Amen!

Monday–after the 4th Sunday in Lent　　　**Reading: Ephesians 2:1-10**

Your Study Notes Regarding the Power of the Past, Present and Future

Write down as many ways as possible you can work within the next 2 weeks to share the story of God's redemptive love with others.

_____

_____

_____

_____

_____

_____

_____

_____

_____

_____

_____

_____

_____

_____

_____

_____

_____

Tuesday—after the 4ᵗʰ Sunday in Lent   **Reading: Psalm 32**

Penitential Pleas and Praise

We all miss the mark at some points in life. What mark is that? It is the mark set before us to live Holy and blameless. Paul in Romans 3:23 simply drives this point home by saying—"all have sinned." In our missing the mark we find ourselves in guilt for wrongdoings, or taking the wrong direction. Often sin translates as willful disobedience, or sometimes it relates to meanness of spirit or viciousness; in other connotations it exists simply as self-deception or even more being the reprobate—that is the hardcore degenerate— at heart.

No matter how we size-up sin though, we do know that God hears our pleas for forgiveness when we acknowledge our disobedience and confess in true penitence. We only need to consult I John 1:9 to verify this fact. The relief that can be realized then leads us from penitence to praise. Thus, happiness can be ours when we surrender the guilt associated with our moral debts. David, King and Psalmist, tells us that after holding on to his sin in silence he was sick "to the bone, per se. Have you ever experienced that kind of deep down punishing, remorseful feeling as a result of holding some guilt within? Truly, it's not a good feeling.

David being "a man after God's own Heart" knew that he could not hide his sin from God. His relationship with God as Father helped him to come to his senses and just admit to God that he had sinned. There are several conclusions that possibly could be inferred that brought him to this point of penitence. We may consider that David as the shepherd son of Jesse discerned that his Kingship had been designed by God who knew everything about him. David as the shepherd boy had experienced that whenever he walked through the valleys of the shadow of death, God was there. He could never move beyond his presence. And David, as the youthful giant slayer, was fully aware that He could trust in the power of God through a sling and a stone to give him victory over evil. David, as the anointed King, knew God too as his Creator; for he recognized that his life was wonderfully and fearfully made, and planned for such a time as this. So in the midst of this "Bathsheba's pregnant, and I had Uriah killed to cover" crisis, he had no choice, but to come face-to-face with his Father God.

Thinking of David's plight and surrender brings to mind how often we sing "I Surrender All," yet we hold on to the guilt of so many things. The hymn encourages us to come to our senses as did David, the reckless prodigal in this situation. It urges us to go to our Father God after we have exhausted his possessions bestowed upon us with wasteful living; finding ourselves perhaps in a worldly pigpen. With genuine repentance however, just like David we too can realize genuine restoration and cry aloud "He restoreth my Soul!" Hallelujah!

Today, meditatively be encouraged to reflect on the thought expressed as the hymn suggests: "All to him I freely give". It is in this type giving—when we come clean with God, then we too can truly be filled with His Holy Spirit. We find that like David the repentant King, we can experience all of the happiness and peace that our "Blessed Savior" can give. In faith and with an intense and willful desire to yield our lives to God, we can expect that our Father God's everlasting grace and mercy will continually enfold us all the days of our lives. And like David the Psalmist, we too can move from penitence to shouts of Praise of our Loving Father, God. Hallelujah! Amen!

Tuesday—after the 4ᵗʰ Sunday in Lent   **Reading: Psalm 32**

Your Study Notes Regarding Penitential Pleas and Praise

What other lessons can you draw from Psalm 32? How does this psalm relate to Psalm 51?

_____

_____

_____

_____

_____

_____

_____

_____

_____

_____

_____

_____

_____

_____

_____

_____

_____

_____

_____

_____

Wednesday—after the 4ᵗʰ Sunday in Lent   **Reading: Numbers 21:4-9**

Prepared for Peace

Recently I read a call for a Missions trip to Africa wherein the organizer asked for specific-trained personnel and interested persons who possessed the quality of being "Happy Campers." I laughed a little at that but quickly was reminded of a more serious concern the organizer probably had. When we do missions work, there is no room for complainers or whiners. God's call to the mission field is not for the faint at heart either. Christian missions work, whether in urban areas, outback, rural, or desert locations calls for resolute dedication to the commitment of outreach and peaceful attitudes.

It is pretty easy to be enthusiastic about being an ambassador for Jesus Christ. Yet it is necessary to be confidently assured of our call to work in the fields where God needs laborers. The call often is to minister to those who may be hurting, to those who have lost hope, or to those who are in need of a Greater Physician to heal a lifetime of emotional and physical pain. Ministry through missions offers our hands, our hearts, our minds and our souls to love our neighbors as God has loved us.

In 2007 The United Methodist Global Missions board produced a DVD to recruit for many areas of church missions. The theme song playing behind each segment in a most beautiful and symphonic sound is the refrain:

> *"Here I am Lord, Is it I Lord? I have heard you calling in the night.*
> *I will go Lord, if you lead me. I will hold your people in my heart."* [47]

Answering God's call is bound to be challenging, whether it is going in the field thousands of miles away or just over to the next city from where we are. Jesus told the seventy to go out, not taking anything significant with them. Yet they came back with glowing reports. God's hand will always be at work when we choose to serve on His behalf. Know that we too can go into the field without complaints as we have a God who will provide.

As we each yearn to grow in the knowledge and grace of our Lord and Savior, consider God's call to go and teach all nations. Consider looking right around where we are to reach out to someone who may need to be baptized this Easter. Seeking people to come for baptism is a great mission field. Let's pray daily that if God calls us beyond our local area, that we can be prepared to say "Here I am, Lord," and truly be a happy ambassador (*camper that is*) for the sake of Jesus Christ!

Wednesday—after the 4ᵗʰ Sunday in Lent   **Reading: Numbers 21:4-9**

Your Study Notes Regarding Preparedness for Peace

Write down a brief description of a memorable experience you have had while working with others in an outreach ministries. If you have not worked on any missions or outreach, jot down the type of mission work for which you think you would most be suited.

_____

_____

_____

_____

_____

_____

_____

_____

_____

_____

_____

_____

_____

_____

_____

_____

_____

_____

Thursday –after the Fourth Sunday in Lent   **Reading: John 3: 14-21**

Pitches and Poles

Several years ago, while leading our church choir, I found a beautiful rendition of John 3:16 in a "Joy for Praise" Songbook.[48] The melody was very simple but required some skilled voice control for the soft approaches and mounting emphases at the end when singing about the "living forever." As the choir gained that control in rehearsing the song, I could see the joy that burst forth from the message among the facial expressions of various choir members. They had mastered the mechanics of the music, and now were being ministered to by the message as they sang.

The spirituality of God's word in song should not be underestimated. We all know that there are many hymns and songs that support the doctrine of scripture. Take for instance the hymn "Lift Him Up", where Jesus' words are repeated—"And if I, if I be lifted up from the earth, I'll draw all men unto me." The hymn writer echoes the idea of Jesus being lifted up for the world to see. Think about Jesus Himself telling Nicodemus to consider that Moses had lifted up the serpent in the wilderness. You find Nicodemus was puzzled about a number of things Jesus had already told him. And Jesus too was amazed that Nicodemus didn't know these things as he was a Teacher in the Temple! So in breaking down the truth of the matter of His divine status, Jesus simply referred Nicodemus back to something he should know about already!

The serpents were a punishment God sent upon the complaining Israelites who voiced, (maybe now since they were on this exodus journey), that Moses should have left them in Egypt. That was a grave sin! And God punished that sin with fiery serpents that bit them and many of them died. Whew! So then, the people realizing the enormity of their sin now are in need of prayer. Sounds familiar? And that is what Moses did! God then answered him by telling Moses to place a brazen serpent upon a pole and to lift it up so as to heal the people.

With this biblical story, we find another composer blends music and this scripture with the old hymn, "Look and Live... look to Jesus now and live." [49] If the people looked upon that raised serpent, they would live. In essence this was a type of salvation not due to looking at the serpent but because of God's steadfast love (Hebrew -*hesed)* and mercy for Israel.

Certainly Jesus was not telling Nicodemus that he was a type of serpent, but the comparison here suggests just as the serpent was lifted on the pole, so would Jesus be lifted up on the cross. And just as the people looked to the brazen serpent to live, so sinners now must look to Jesus for their salvation.

If we look upon Jesus, we too can live because of God's steadfast love and mercy. John 3:16 validates just how long we can live: Forever! Today we can think further on the value of how sacred songs and hymns enhance understanding and offer a deeper revelation of scriptures; we can think on how the music give us melodious and harmonious feelings of the joy that are entwined within the Word of God. Sometimes these songs may break down the theology into simple statements of faith, in the same manner as Jesus did for Nicodemus! I think the expressions I saw that night on the faces of the choir illustrated theology being caught.

Thus I share today with you a simple message of salvation— "Look and live" my friends. Look to Jesus now and live! Each of us should endeavor to break down that message of salvation and tell someone who really needs to know that "whoever believes in Him shall live, Forever!" Amen!

Thursday –after the Fourth Sunday in Lent   **Reading: John 3: 14-21**

Your Study Notes Regarding Pitches and Poles

List a few songs that you know that offer simple scriptural insights. Make a few notes on the insight from your study of John 3:14-21.

---

8)C8

FACT: Today, two serpent motifs are commonly used to symbolize the practice and profession of medicine. Internationally, the most popular symbol of medicine is the single serpent–entwined staff of Asklepios (Latin, Aesculapius), the ancient Greco-Roman god of medicine. However, in the United States, the staff of Asklepios (the Asklepian), and a double serpent–entwined staff with surmounting wings (the caduceus) are both popular medical symbols. The latter symbol is often designated as the "medical caduceus" and is equated with the ancient caduceus, the double serpent-entwined staff of the Greco-Roman god Hermes (Latin, Mercury)

Source: Ann Intern Med. 2003; 138:673-677.
http://www.annals.org/cgi/reprint/138/8/673.pdf

Author's Note: Is it possible Moses' Pole was the very first symbol of the healing profession? Perhaps the claim for origin of the medical motifs should be based on Numbers 21:6. (Selah!)

8)C8

Friday–after the 4th Sunday in Lent   **Ephesians 1: 3-14;**

Prayer on a Positioned Pathway

Here is a fact: "Because of our position as believers in Jesus Christ, we are blessed with divine privileges and spiritual assets unimaginable." The Apostle Paul confirms this fact in his message to the Ephesians to the praise of God's glory. Can we assimilate exactly what this means for as we strive to walk in paths of righteousness? If the answer is yes, then there is more reason to give thanks. If the answer is no, then there is more reason to pray for further understanding of who we are as Believers in Jesus Christ.

Why not take time today to thank God in as many ways as Paul unfolds these spiritual blessings. Why? Because we are in relationship with Jesus Christ and the Holy Spirit is active in our lives. When we pray fervently and with deep desire, the Holy Spirit will intercede to reveal to us and set us free to understand better our position on this pathway of life.

So here is Paul's outline for each of us to pray:

I thank you Lord, for every spiritual blessing you've given me in the heavenly places.

I thank you Lord for having chosen me to be holy and blameless before you in love.

I thank you for having destined me for adoption as your child through Christ Jesus.

I thank you for the glorious grace you freely bestow upon me through your beloved Son Jesus Christ.

I thank you for the redemption I have through the blood of Jesus.

I thank you for the forgiveness of my trespasses according to the riches of your grace of Christ Jesus.

I thank you Lord for having made known to me the mystery of your will set forth in Christ.

I thank you Lord for the inheritance I have obtained according to your purpose, counsel and will.

I thank you Lord for my life to the praise of your Glory.

I thank you Lord for having been marked with the seal of the promised Holy Spirit when I heard the Word of Truth, the gospel of your Salvation, and believed in Christ Jesus.
I thank you Lord for the Holy Spirit as the pledge of my redemption as your own to the praise of your Glory. Amen!

"Now unto Him who is able to do exceedingly, abundantly above all that I ask or think, according to the power that works in me, to Him be glory in the church by Christ Jesus to all generations, forever and ever, Amen." [50]

Friday–after the 4th Sunday in Lent   **Ephesians 1: 3-14;**

Your Study Notes Regarding Prayer and Positioned Pathways

List as many Spiritual Blessings as possible that you have been able to recognize that have come into your life. Date each if you can remember when they occurred. Make a note if you prayed specifically for any one of these.

_____

_____

_____

_____

_____

_____

_____

_____

_____

_____

_____

_____

_____

_____

_____

_____

_____

_____

_____

Saturday –after the 4ᵗʰ Sunday in Lent   **Reading: Isaiah 43:16-21**

Phrasing a Plain Petition

Sometimes songs ring in our minds as prayers. One morning recently I found myself concluding my prayer with the phrase: Fix Me Jesus! Fix Me. You see my prayers were centered on renewing my mind. "Fix me Jesus" implores God to do a new thing with the brokenness of life now in need of repair. The phrase "Fix Me Jesus" as I know it however, comes from a traditional African-American spiritual which still speaks to the need we have for much of our contemporary brokenness. Yet, consider there is a modern cliché that so often supports us when we are in denial— "if ain't broke, don't fix it." We sometimes evade those breached areas of our lives, by looking the other way with the elusion of "it ain't broke!" Truly we deceive ourselves.

But our faithful and righteous ancestors knew better from their harsh survival of being in bondage that there was a need to just pray: "Fix Me Jesus, Fix Me. And even more interesting you find it was in song nonetheless that the prayer was consummated to focus not even on the present or former things, but the things yet to come:

"Fix me for my heavenly home, Fix me Jesus, Fix Me.
Fix me for my long white robe, Fix me Jesus, Fix Me.
Fix me for my journey home, Fix me Jesus, Fix Me,
Fix me for my dying bed, Fix me Jesus Fix, Me"

It is probable many of these captive souls did not have a handle on any more eloquent words to express their needs. Yet for all of the brokenness and abuses of life they experienced, they understood Jesus could fix it. He could do a new thing beyond this present life. This phraseology seemed to be a covering of all things and all sins. Fixing, repairing, renewing, a new destiny certainly was a need of the masses who desired to either survive or move on to a better world.

"Fix me Jesus" is still in our times today a simple and plain prayer. It is a simple starting point in asking for the remedy of all our needs. Looking to the cross of redemption, or even further to the resurrection of Christ, we can claim this new thing that God can make visible in repairing and renewing our lives. But we would need to come face-to-face with God in a Spirit of brokenness, and be sincerely repentant as we pray. Then I would urge that we could continue in prayerful petition just as part of the A.M.E. prayer of Confession concludes saying:

"We do earnestly repent, and are heartily sorry...Forgive us all that is past and grant that we may ever hereafter serve and please you in newness of life, to the honor and glory of your name, through Jesus Christ our Lord. Amen."

You know I can still hear the voices of those old gospel choirs from days gone by singing that beautiful melody: "Fix me for my Heavenly home, Fix me Jesus, fix me!" Can you hear it? It's a plain and most simple petition: "Fix me Jesus..., fix me!"

Saturday –after the 4ᵗʰ Sunday in Lent   **Reading: Isaiah 43:16-21**

Your Study Notes Regarding Phrasing a Plain Petition

What common plea do you find you use most often in prayer? What has God done in your life that you would consider a "new thing"?

_____

_____

_____

_____

_____

_____

_____

_____

_____

_____

_____

_____

_____

_____

_____

_____

_____

_____

_____

_____

The Pervasive Price

"...for a feast is made for friendship; ...for a feast is made for fellowship."-Matthew Henry Complete Bible Commentary

I would suggest that the work of two contemporary Gospel artists could offer a convergent musical view of a rich Biblical setting—the great feast at the house of Mary and Martha of Bethany. There is Richard Smallwood's "At the Table" which offers a joyous hand-clapping gospel shuffle invitation in song to: "Come over here, where the table is spread!" [51] On the other hand, Cece Winans' meditative ballad "Alabaster Box" [52] might encourage us to contemplatively read and re-read Mary's experience with Jesus in this leading up to His final days in Jerusalem.

John, a most devoted disciple of Jesus recorded that many who had gone to Jerusalem leading up to the Passover looked with much curiosity for Jesus -that is post his recent Miracle. It was six days before the Passover, when Jesus and other disciples came to supper at Bethany. Lazarus was now alive again—that is resurrected from the dead, and sat at the table. Jesus too was at the table. Martha served the supper. Mary sat at Jesus' feet opening her alabaster box which contained a pound of expensive and most fragrant oil. After all of the mourning and weeping for Lazarus, imagine this setting— all must have seemed like it was an amazing dream! As the table was spread, you probably could imagine that this had to be a very joyous occasion—like-"Joy over here, where the table is spread!" And just as it happens with many celebrations of family and friends these days, likewise back then someone had to start a spat: here infusing a rebuke of Mary was Judas Iscariot—holder and thief of the common purse and ultimate betrayer.

Seeing that Mary had begun to pour the spikenard to anoint Jesus' feet, Judas' scolding about its value had little to do with his pretense of worry for the poor. And Mary perhaps had already internalized quite some time before this supper that it was her duty to be at Jesus' feet—out of love for Him; out of devotion to Him; moreover out of gratitude. So as others were gathered at the table, one could imagine that this disruption to the peace and love that pervaded the room was an annoyance, and Jesus Himself spoke to neutralize Judas' complaint. "Leave her alone!"

Jesus knew, and Mary knew the price of what was to come, and now nothing more mattered as she may have felt it was *all* to Him she now owed. Three hundred denarii, as Judas alleged, would never be the real cost of that precious oil Mary so selflessly offered to prepare Jesus for the day of his burial. Judas in his selfish and self-serving guile had no idea of the price of what was to come. The cost at stake sat here at the table; not only was the Master's life, but also Lazarus' life too a part of the Jews treacherous plot. Death on a cross—that was an incalculable price.

And because of that most merciful act, just like Lazarus, we too have been called out of bondage, unbound and set free. We should be ever so grateful for Jesus' power to bring us back from episodes of spiritual deaths; episode that may have had our lives at some points bound and perhaps even putrefied like Lazarus' was. As we now can sit at the table with Jesus, we must rid ourselves of cunning and greed for worldly riches –the mind of Judas. Our gratitude to Him should keep us subservient just the same as Mary and Martha rejoiced in his loving presence. Like Mary, we can pour out our praise to Jesus similarly as she poured oil out of the alabaster box: drenching Him freely.

In approaching His coming Passion, we are reminded to share our loving thankfulness to Jesus likewise. We do this by letting others know there is no quantifiable cost for His mercy. We too must remember to invite them along on the journey by telling them: "He's over here, where the table is spread and the feast of the Lord is going on! "

Sunday-the Fifth Sunday in Lent   *Reading:* **John 12:1-11**

Your Study Notes Regarding The Pervasive Price

Make notes on why you think it was important to Jesus to sit at supper in Bethany. List any merciful acts from others bestowed upon you at some point in your life that you could not repay.

_____

_____

_____

_____

_____

_____

_____

_____

_____

_____

_____

_____

_____

_____

_____

_____

_____

_____

_____

Monday–after the 5th Sunday in Lent　　　　**Reading: Philippians 3:4b-14**

Freedom to Pursue the Prize

"I am free, praise the Lord I'm free, no longer bound, no more chains holding me. My Soul is resting, it's just a blessing. Praise the Lord, Hallelujah I'm free".-Traditional African American

It is noted that Rev. Milton Brunson, one of the first organizers of what would become known as Mass Gospel Choirs, passed away from this life in 1997. It seems although he had been ill, his death was quite unexpected by those who were friends or avid listeners to his music. Through powerful praise in song, he and the Thompson Community Singers offered the message of this African American gospel song: *"I am free, praise the Lord, I'm free."* At the point of his death and transition, suddenly he now was free. Yet Rev. Brunson left a near 50 year legacy of the gospel sounds for the world to share.

The power of a song that moves one to tears or some other expressive emotion is often indescribable. This is the kind of expression, and in a sense freedom we find demonstrated in Rev. Brunson's ministry of the song and other gospel greats whose music moved people to different levels of worship. So it is understandable when we feel the Power of Christ working within that we are left with an emotive feeling that is overwhelming and beyond words. This is the kind of power that can free us, so like the Apostle Paul we can count all things lost. Things we thought were gainful can often become the unwanted burdens that "so easily beset us." They hinder our progress as we strive to pursue Christ. Yet when we pursue the power of Christ, our beings are freed up to no longer be bound by those weights; in essence, no more chains holding us. We in turn "Praise the Lord," through the expression of "Hallelujah," for that freedom. We thank God as perhaps then we understand better too how Jesus, our Savior through the power of the Holy Spirit broke the chains of death's bondage and freed all. Hallelujah!

But the question comes: "How do we come to a point of understanding that power, and the need to be freed?" One United Methodist

110

Prayer of Confession and Pardon urges us to pray: "Free us for joyful obedience, through Jesus Christ our Lord." Knowing the Power of Christ's resurrection can free us to be obedient. There are numerous promises in the Word of God tied to obedience. Keeping our eyes on Christ helps us to be obedient. Think of Peter when he doubted looking at the boisterous wind after Christ without hesitation had already bid him to, "Come." Jesus' sustaining and freeing power was sufficient, supplying him supernatural power; had Peter been obedient he may have reached the Master.

Accordingly, to gain Christ through obedience is also to gain the freedom we need to pursue the gifts that God has in store for each of us. To know Christ is to experience the power of His resurrection—which was in its essence, total freedom! The scriptures provide much instruction on ways in which we can pursue Christ through His own power. We could search and find that

- Jesus Himself teaches us to know the Truth, as it is the Truth that can make us free. (John 8:31-32)
- Freedom in Christ means also there are no confines with the Spirit.
- There are no physical restraints in freedom. Circumcision of the Jews was a symbolic cutting away of the physical flesh that would act as restraint to be a true child of God. When we are free from things that physically bind us, we know our true identity in Christ Jesus.
- Being free through the power of Christ, we are liberated to be transformed into new creations (2 Corinthians 5:17).
- Consider Jesus' exegesis on the freedom of being born of the Spirit as he answered Nicodemus' questions. (John 3: 8)
- Where the Spirit of the Lord is, there is liberty (2 Corinthians 3:17)

Simply opening the mind to accept new truths can be a transforming freedom. Think of how Christ opened the minds of His disciples and the men on the Emmaus Road with His expository sermons about Himself, the Messiah (Luke 24:27). Spending time in communion with God through the liberty of the Holy Spirit can offer us regeneration. Listening or singing, let us continue in the way of those that have ministered powerfully before the Lord. I'd expect that they were free to lift up their praises like never before; releasing the bonds, which in turn freed them for Joyful Obedience. Jesus wants us to be free as He is free. Today we should find a place of solitude so as to free our minds for a short period of time. And while we are in that quiet place, furthermore, know that God wants us to be free to sense the presence of His Holy Spirit in that space.

Monday–after the 5th Sunday in Lent   **Reading: Philippians 3:4b-14**

Your Study Notes on Freedom to Pursue the Prize

Describe a time in your life that you have felt totally free in the Holy Spirit.
Have you ever felt totally bound by a situation?

_____

_____

_____

_____

_____

_____

_____

_____

_____

_____

_____

_____

_____

_____

_____

_____

_____

_____

Providence and Provisions

Growing up in lower South Carolina, I remember from my childhood the joyous singing of the hymn "Bringing in the Sheaves!" And although there was a hint in the stanzas that this was an agricultural theme-based song, I always wondered "what were the sheaves?" There were many church services, and the once a year event of the "Harvest Festivals" where I know for sure, this hymn was sung. Of course by singing all stanzas and the refrain repeatedly, many of us kids were worn out by the time we got down to the final "we will come rejoicing"! And we would stare each other down with that look of "are we not through yet?"

Now as I think back on those Sundays, and the fact that many of the older generation of that community of faith were mostly farmers who eked out the best of a living for their families, planting crops and gardens, the familiarity and joy of singing that hymn makes more sense! But moving further into the thought process, the oldest members of this church community like many others in the south were freed children and grandchildren of a people who had been born into or held captive, figuratively in the Babylon in America. These were people who joyously brought the jars of canned vegetables and fruit, broad leaves of freshly picked collard greens, turnips and rutabagas; ripe ears of corn bound with husks, sweet potatoes; and my grandmother would supply pots of billowing ferns, all to cover and decorate the altar to celebrate the service of the "Harvest Festival" every end of the year!

These celebrations I now look back on as having been such a wholesome time in my life. It was a time of singing and much laughter and chatter among the people. Each community rejoiced in fervent worship services with celebrated prayer and preaching, roll calling of local churches that were represented to support, raising of the highest "collection," and a giving of the harvest to those who were in need. They celebrated with thankfulness all the very great things God had done in their lives year after year. Moreover, with the sharing of the Harvest, they did not forget those who were still burdened with the lack of necessities. It seems now that back then God had gathered His church to rejoice, forgetting the toils, and tears that might have been sown in fret of a poor harvest, or lack of provisions that accompanied sharecropping or simple farming. The gathering itself was the time of harvest, the fellowship in worship was the time of rejoicing. It was a joyful celebration for God's providing for and delivering His people one more year, and they were actually bringing in the sheaves!

God's providence and deliverance still remains today as it did during those years of my childhood, and as it did many thousands of years before. Many of us still may sow seeds of tears as all these years later, we at present perhaps may face different circumstances in lack of resources, or as we often may shoulder burdens sometimes seemingly unbearable. We may simply just find ourselves in what Dr. David Jeremiah describes as the "Cul-de-Sacs of life," [52]–those places where we do not find real joy. But know that we can reap a great harvest of life everlasting, when we are "sowing for the Master, sowing seeds of kindness." Christ has guaranteed and sealed these mercies, that no matter how long the suffering, or sorrow, there will be a great harvest of joy! And truly we will sing to the Glory of God, and be filled with much more laughter than experienced in those "Harvest" days now gone by. Truly in that great harvest day "we shall come rejoicing, bringing in the sheaves!" Amen!

Tuesday –after the 5ᵗʰ Sunday in Lent   **Reading: Psalm 126**

Your Study Notes Regarding Providence and Provisions:

After reading Psalm 126, describe one of your life experiences that aligns with the Psalmist's themes of deliverance and God's mercy. Make note of any time you have felt like you were dreaming when something really good happened for you?

_____

_____

_____

_____

_____

_____

_____

_____

_____

_____

_____

_____

_____

_____

_____

_____

_____

_____

Wednesday –after the 5ᵗʰ Sunday in Lent   **Reading: Hebrews 5:5-10;**

The Perfect Priest –the Perfect Provision

The sounds and scenes from a charismatic worship service captured on DVD that I recently watched sticks in my mind. The camera pans across worshippers in this sanctuary as many are on their knees, some with outstretched arms while others are bowed reverently in prayer, praise, tears, and humility; at the same time the singers, powerfully yet tenderly minister in the background songs of Gods' love. One of the most beautiful and moving songs sung in their medley, *"Oh How He Loves You and Me"* brings an intensified aura of holiness to the setting.[54] I thought here is a scene of people waiting before God, waiting in and on His Holy Spirit; waiting for the power of God to descend upon them as God's presence inhabits their prayers and praises. The scene is not one we will find in traditional or mainstream worship services on an ongoing basis; it may be occasionally, or not at all. Yet, the sensed holiness of worship exhibited during this particular experience pointed to the willingness of those worshippers to bow down, their willingness to let go, and their willingness to let God have His way while they were in His presence. What a preparation it seemed for entering the "Holy of Holies!"

Jesus, our eternal and compassionate High Priest offered intense cries and tears to God as He bowed down in the Garden of Gethsemane knowing He would be the sacrifice, "once for ALL [people] when He offered up Himself." It was there in the garden that He prayed, "not my will, but Yours be done." God chose Jesus to be the eternal High priest. "Jesus also for a short while was made "a little lower than the angels just like man. But because He submitted to death, He is now crowned with glory and splendor. By God's grace he had to experience death for all mankind."[55]

Meditating deeply on the song "Oh How He Loves You and Me" may accordingly bring us to passionate tears, and help us to ponder further on just <u>how</u> profound a thing it is that Jesus, the Perfect Priest and the Perfect Provision gave His life for us.

Oh, how he loves you and me,
Oh, how he loves you and me,
He gave His life, what more could he give;
Oh, how He loves you, oh, how He Loves Me,
Oh, how He loves you and me.
Jesus to Calvary did go, His love for the whole world to show;
What he did there, brought hope from despair.
Oh how He loves you, oh, how He Loves Me,
Oh, how He loves you and me.

We say "Jesus died for me" and we know He laid down His life. But, what does that really mean to each of us? Truly as the song corroborates, what He did there at Calvary, that act of love did bring hope to mankind! As the sin-bearer, taking on the complete wrath of God that was reserved for sinful man, Jesus' willingness to die on Calvary provided for mankind an escape route from "bondage by death and Satan." Think of Isaac, Abraham's only son on the altar about to be sacrificed. Think of Jesus as He on the cross of Calvary is in the flesh the symbolic substitute of that more worthy ram seen in the thicket by Abraham. Any one of us could be named Isaac. Oh, what love God has provided to rescue us! Out of this despairing situation, Jesus made available a rightful way for us to come into God's presence. The Lord Jesus Himself also declared that "I am the Door," since man is now delivered out of the wrath; "I am the Way," the doorway by which anyone who entered would be able ultimately to receive the crown of Glory God intended for Man to have. Think not only on His death as what He did for us, but also see that "Deliver us from evil" is the granted result of the power of Jesus' resurrection.

When we truly discover and comprehend the magnitude of this expression of love, it becomes very easy to tell others: ***"Oh** how he loves you and me!"* We then truly realize *"What a friend we have in Jesus!"* He is the friend who laid down his life for a friend: you and me. Thus maybe we see even more clearly in His dying and God's perfect provision how much He really loves you and me!" Let's be challenged and willing to bow down in God's presence today wherever we are. Let us be challenged and willing to wait in His Presence for His Holy Spirit and for his provisions. While waiting let's just hum prayerfully *"Oh how He loves you and me..."* to experience the Shekinah beauty of God's Holiness; and simultaneously pray that through His provision of Jesus the Perfect Priest, He may perform His endless atoning work in us! Amen!

Wednesday –after the 5ᵗʰ Sunday in Lent Reading: Hebrews 5:5-10;

Your Study Notes Regarding the Perfect Priest—the Perfect Provision

How do you understand better Jesus role as Priest, and how He enables you to enter boldly into God's presence? Read the Genesis 22:1-14 text and make notes as well.

_____

_____

_____

_____

_____

_____

_____

_____

_____

_____

_____

_____

_____

_____

_____

_____

_____

_____

Thursday –after the 5ᵗʰ Sunday in Lent   **Reading: Philippians 3:4b-14**

Greater Passions Yield Greater Privileges

A beautiful song composed some years ago by one of America's greatest Gospel songwriters, Dr. Margaret Pleasant Douroux, expresses the celebration that the Apostle Paul keeps central in his letter to the Philippians: *Count It All Joy*! Dr. Douroux's phrasing simply states:

"I count everything as Joy in Christ Jesus; I count everything as Joy in the Lord.
All vict'ries I share, all the burdens I bear,
Everything! Everything! Everything in Christ is Joy!

The worth of summing up all things we experience in life as joy has to be reinforced by the premise that it is our passions for Christ—to know Him more intimately, and to urge others to identify with Him too, that will yield us greater privileges; not only now in this present life, but also in our life hereafter. Through our confidence in Christ alone and the power of His Resurrection, we should be able to count our adversities, and our good fortunes as anchors in the sea of joy! In our humanness however, we find that this is not an easy "row to hoe" per se. How do we look in the face of hardships and rejoice about it? In our own strength we cannot. But if and when we rely only on the power of Christ Jesus to turn the unfavorable things that happen in our lives to good, then we really can do all things through His strength! Being able to accept the good, the bad and the undesirable things of life with an air of joyful optimism is a virtue only He can give us. When we accept and exhibit this power in our lives, truly God gets the Glory and that for us too is Joy!!.

What is this confidence in Christ and the Power of His resurrection that we should rely upon? We must consciously and humbly accept that we cannot trust our own self-help attitudes. This kind of trust often causes the summing up of what we think is gain or privilege to become the weight of more burdens. When we manipulate outcomes of circumstances in life based on our own desires, versus asking God's will to be done, we often arrive at destinations of empty dreams, lackluster desires and often times great loss. In contrast, we must be persuaded beyond the shadow of a doubt inwardly to know that it is Jesus alone, through the grace of God, who holds the all-encompassing power to help us in our time of need. He pronounced to all that with His resurrection, He forever lives now holding the Keys of the unseen realm and of death. That is the Power of His Resurrection. Thus it is He who is the beginning of God's will in our lives when we humbly come to the end of ourselves.

How can we practically invite and sustain this confidence and power into our lives? Consider the pattern of the ideals such as Glenn Burleigh offered in the song "Order My Steps." First we ask God to keep our pathway ordered with His Word. Secondly, we commit to being still, while God is working on our behalf. Thirdly, we invite the Holy Spirit to help us bridle our tongues and to help us embrace only words that edify those things that are good and pure! When we add up each day the blessings that come along with this kind of power, the sum total can only be joy.

As we approach the time of Passion in this year's Lenten journey, let us hold close these ideals in prayer to help us stay anchored in Joy. Let us pray inwardly for greater passions to share in Christ's passion—that is His suffering, death, and resurrection, leaving behind the minutiae of worldly confidence. Just as Christ died, surrendering His Spirit in confidence to the Father, let us humble our own wills with such trust, knowing we will experience His resurrection power which yields for us greater joy here and now. Let us be mindful to know this joy does not equal perfection, but will yield far greater privileges as we pursue the prize of eternity. Count it all as Joy! Amen.

Thursday –after the 5ᵗʰ Sunday in Lent   **Reading: Philippians 3:4b-14**

Your Study Notes Regarding Passions and Privileges

What confidences do you have in Christ and the Power of His resurrection? Do you rely solely on this confidence?

_____

_____

_____

_____

_____

_____

_____

_____

_____

_____

_____

_____

_____

_____

_____

_____

_____

_____

_____

_____

_____

Friday –after the 5ᵗʰ Sunday in Lent   **Reading: Psalm 118:1-2, 19-29**

Passage to the Passover

Imagine this: Christ and His entourage are heading up to Jerusalem. This is the time of the Passover when the pilgrims traditionally travel to the Great Worship, similarly as they had journeyed in the past for other great feasts of God! Some historians note that there are four thousand steps up to the top of Mount Sinai. You see Jesus has been walking from Jericho just in the past days which is just as far below sea level as Jerusalem is above sea level. You might kind of compare the height of Jerusalem to that of Denver, Colorado—you know, "Mile High"- to get a general idea of how high the city sat upon the hill! It is no wonder that the people rejoiced when they could see the Gates of the Temple. There is no wonder that they would be encouraged to sing the liturgies as they *"entered into His gates with Thanksgiving."* To enter at the "Gates of Righteousness" is truly ceremonial to the pilgrimage that arrives.

So it is not by chance that the Psalmists throughout wrote the songs of solemn thanksgiving for the many blessings that God had provided them along the journey and also in granting them a safe arrival. However, the local people, according to the custom of that time, would come out of the city to greet the dignitary. So in our vision of this passage, think of how many of those in the crowd have come out to accompany Jesus to the place of honor He will visit inside of the city. Along the way, there is a festive ring

ෂාⅭℛ

The Gates of Righteousness historically represents the place of arrival wherein the Jewish pilgrims who were headed to the Passover would have to ask for entry into the Temple. They were the massive, ornate temple gates that led respectively from the Court of the Gentiles to the Court of the Women (the one known in Jesus' time as the Beautiful Gate), and from the Court of the Women (so-called because no woman could go beyond it) to the Court of Israel (the one known in Jesus' time as the Nicanor Gate); They were called "the gates of righteousness" because they were shut against all who were not covenant people.
References: (1) Wycliffe's Bible Commentary, Moody Press, (2)http://passthetoast.wordpress.com/sermons/

ෂාⅭℛ

124

of songs and praises. It may be that the spirit of these songs of the people compare to the fervor of the way we sing contemporary praise songs like: *"This is the Day! This is the day that the Lord hath made!"* [56] Or, the gospel version of Glenn Burleigh's composed song *"Oh Magnify"* – *"O Magnify the Lord with me. Let us exalt His name together...We will rejoice and be glad."* [57]

There are shouts of joy and gladness as this is no routine entry into Jerusalem they are partaking. It is indeed a Triumphal Entry, and the people are rejoicing and shouting "Save now, I pray O Lord" that translates similarly in Hebrew to "Hosanna, Hosanna." You see with the news of the recent miracles, they now believe and acknowledge that Jesus is Lord!! They understand that Salvation is here!! They are praising in the streets because "Deliverance" is at hand in the person of Jesus, the Messiah. You see the Good News is here in their presence:

"He's come to set the Captives free—Salvation!
He's come to make the blind to see—Salvation!
And the government will be upon His shoulders—Salvation!
Salvation is here! Salvation is here this day!" [58]

Our own understanding of this triumphal day in the history of Israel, and the use of the Prophetic words in the Psalms is so far removed in time. It may be hard to assimilate the connectivity. Yet it would behoove each of us to align our hearts with the Psalmist's expression of thanksgiving for deliverance just as the people did on the road to Jerusalem. As we know now, Psalm 118 is at the literal center of God's Word; as we desire Christ to be our eternal center we can agree in our own solo voice similarly to the cantor at the temple, *"Open to me Lord, the gates of your righteousness."* We also can apply the shouts of Hosanna to our own lives now: Save us Lord! And furthermore, although the rulers of Israel rejected Jesus the Messiah as His Kingship would not fit in their plans, we can accept him as the chief cornerstone in our lives. So today let us consider ourselves blessed, as we have another opportunity to raise our voice in thanks to the Lord with all the people throughout the ages! We can rejoice and be glad for surely His Salvation endures forever! Amen!

Friday—after the 5ᵗʰ Sunday in Lent **Reading: Psalm 118:1-2, 19-29**

Your Study Notes Regarding Passage to the Passover

Did you know Zechariah predicted Jesus' entry into Jerusalem just as it happened? See Zechariah 9:9 and make notes. What passions do you realize you have for Jesus that makes you rejoice in His presence?

_____

_____

_____

_____

_____

_____

_____

_____

_____

_____

_____

_____

_____

_____

_____

_____

Saturday –after the 5ᵗʰ Sunday in Lent   **Reading: Philippians 2:5-11**

Pedagogy for Praising that Precious Name

With much beauty in the melody of the music, we will find a worshipful song composed by Naida Hearn which praises the Name above all names: Jesus!

"Jesus, Name above all names, Beautiful Savior, glorious Lord, Emmanuel, God is with us, Blessed Redeemer, Living Word." [59]

God conferred upon Him the name Jesus, meaning Yahweh is Salvation, which is above all other names. And moreover as Jesus lived His mortal life in complete obedience to God, He humbly completed His mission on earth as the prophesied Suffering Servant. As a result, God would exalt His name above all others. In Jesus therefore is all and He is Lord above all. When we look at His attributes woven into this song, we can find many reasons for which we too should worship Him, whose Name is above all names.

Let us consider first that Jesus is the "radiance of the glory of God." Thus He is the ***Beautiful Savior*** we honor as our Lord of all, who willingly gave up the glory of Heaven to live, suffer and die here on earth. This selfless passion would provide the way of salvation for each of us who would earnestly repent, confess and believe in Him; and it would provide a way for each of us to make all effort to emulate the mind of Christ –a self-sacrificing mind always seeking God's will. As a Beautiful Savior we honor Jesus as He is the Blessed Son of God and second manifestation of the God-head (Father, Son, and Holy Spirit) who shows us the beauty of a Holy creation. Saving us morning by morning, His creative mercies are renewed in our lives daily and also manifested in the beauty of the earth, the heavens, the seas, and the skies.

As ***Glorious Lord***, we know Jesus as King of Kings, Lord of Lords, and our Adonai. On the Mount of Moriah, Abraham experienced our Glorious Lord as the ram in the bush, and the God who Provides—Jehovah-Jireh! On that same mount hundreds of years later, in the beauty of the temple following King Solomon's' prayer of dedication, Solomon and all the people experienced our Glorious Lord when His presence as King of Kings, in the form of divine fire filled the place. We praise Jesus our Glorious Lord in these present moments for filling our earthly temples of clay with the divine fire of His Holy Spirit. We praise and worship our Glorious Lord, for we know in His provisions for us "He is good, and His Mercy endures forever."

As *Emmanuel*, we honor Jesus for being our God who is with us! We honor Emmanuel as His name prophesied by Isaiah and spoken by the Lord's Angel Gabriel to reveal Him as the Son of God. We honor Emmanuel as the incarnate God who abides with us, divine yet human. In being with us, Jesus has promised us that He would never leave us or forsake us. For that we give God praise.

Seeing that Jesus is our *Blessed Redeemer*, we give honor because after His baptism His redemptive mission began and the heavens tore open to bear witness. In His death upon a cross, He affirmed "It is finished" and the earth tore open giving the victory over death. Our Blessed Redeemer got up from the grave just as He said having paid the ransom to deliver perpetually the poor, the brokenhearted, the captives, the blind and the oppressed. Oh what a Redeemer! Along with the psalmists throughout the ages we glorify our Blessed Redeemer as we, coming from the north, south, east and west sing and echo the hymn of praise "Let the redeemed of the Lord say so!" *(Psalm 107:2)*

In our human existence, we can never thank God enough for Jesus our *Living Word*. We continually do our utmost to worship Him the *Logos* of Life in "Spirit and in Truth." We affirm the truth that He was in the beginning the Word; the Living Word that was with God and the Living Word that was God. And as that Living Word, we praise Jesus as He has crowned mankind through the ages with wisdom and power. We worship Jesus as the Living Word, "the two-edged sword which pierces through even the division of our spirits and souls," to discern the most miniscule thoughts and intentions of our hearts. We praise the Living Word whose power is capable of divinely permeating our whole being, bringing us to our knees, and penetrating our tongues enabling us to confess this Name

God has given to be above all other names. We praise Jesus' name because there is no other name given by which we can be saved!

Let us pray: Lord Jesus today, as we prepare our hearts to lay down our palms and coats to pave the way for your entry into our individual "Jerusalems," please accept our praises to your most worthy Name. We continually will praise your Lordship over our lives and praise your name Jesus forevermore! Amen!

Saturday –after the 5th Sunday in Lent   **Reading: Philippians 2:5-11**

Your Study Notes Regarding Pedagogy for Praising that Precious Name

Make a list of songs or hymns that come to mind that sing the praises of Jesus name. After meditating on the scripture reading and being in prayer, call out aloud the name "Jesus" adding each attribute given here in today's reading. Describe your experience!

_____

_____

_____

_____

_____

_____

_____

_____

_____

_____

_____

_____

_____

_____

_____

_____

_____

_____

_____

Palm Sunday –the Sixth Sunday in Lent
Liturgy of the Palm and Passion: *Psalm 31:9-16, Psalm 118:1-2; 19-29*

Palm Sunday- A Preparation for Persecution

The **Passion** *of Christ is a topical description that refers to "his notorious suffering and painful, public death by crucifixion"* [60]

Jesus starts this week of Palms and Passion with what is termed a "Triumphal Entry" and ends it with Him humbling Himself in obedience to the point of death, "even the death of the cross." At this time He enters the city not on the "milk white horse," but on the back of a lowly beast of burden; a donkey that never before had been ridden; the same kind of animal that brought His mother Mary into the town of Bethlehem. There is a crowd of disciples, more commonly thought of as followers who are excited about this "Jesus;" this prophet from Nazareth of Galilee. People now know from the signs and miraculous events that this prophet must be the Messiah. As prophesied, He is healing people of their physical sicknesses and more. It is a great commotion on this day. Envision people shouting: "Ride on King Jesus!" You also see the multitudes spread their clothing on the road while others cut down branches of Palm trees or boughs of leafy trees spreading them on the road as Jesus approached. Many of them may now realize literally the four hundred year-old prophecy of the prophets Zechariah and Isaiah to be this moment in time that the "people in darkness" had so long awaited:

"Rejoice greatly, O daughter of Zion
Shout, O daughter of Jerusalem!
Behold your King is coming to you,
He is just and having salvation,
Lowly, and riding on a donkey,
a colt, the foal of a donkey." [61]

Just imagine you hear the people shout and rejoice as He passes along the way. Imagine their songs of joy sounding much like a tune we now sing: *"This is the Day, this is the Day that the Lord Hath made, I will rejoice, I will rejoice and be glad in it."*

In your mind's ear, hear them singing:

"I will lift up my voice with thanksgiving in my heart! I will lift up my voice with praise!
Hosanna, Blessed Be the Rock, Blessed Be the Rock of my Salvation"[62]

Yes! Along the road, the people sing Hosanna meaning "Save Us" as they "Behold" their King coming unto them. In the background the enemies of the King scoff, and charge Him to quiet His disciples. He sternly derides them with a "surely you jest" kind of reply, as their muteness would send an alarm to all of creation, triggering the rocks to cry out in praise of Him!

However this King is preparing for another type of salvation. Their King is not coming to bring on a war in this earthly realm, but He is headed to battle the powers of the darkness and principalities. He is not riding into Jerusalem as the King the people wanted to overthrow the oppressive rule or to rise up against Rome, but as the Suffering Servant of God the Father and as the Jehovah-Shalom! Entering Jerusalem, *Jesus knows* He will be led to the slaughter to become the sin offering. *Jesus knows* He will be in complete submission to the will of the Father; knowing he must drink from the cup of agony as He would pray in Gethsemane. *Jesus knows* that the Chief leaders will reject Him, and He weeps for Jerusalem, as she will be broken and left desolate, as these stiff-necked people had murdered prophets before Him, and certainly did not want Him to reign over them. *Jesus knows* His sacrificial death will be glorified by the Father. Yes, *Jesus knows* the hour had come when He, the Son of Man would be glorified, and more specifically the name of the Father would be glorified.

During this week of Passion, how do we as Christians, followers of Christ, prepare to suffer with Christ? We are urged to consider several ways: we let the mind of Christ be ours; we check our selfishness, our own self interests and desires at the foot of the cross, as we might be called upon to take up that cross and carry it just like Simon of Cyrene. [63] We weep as Jesus wept for those who would reject salvation; we put on the armor of God to fight against the powers of wickedness in high places. Moreover, we prepare our hearts through tarrying in prayer and fasting so as to be able to answer when Jesus asks each of us: "Are you able to be crucified with me?"

***Palm Sunday* –the Sixth Sunday in Lent**
Liturgy of the Palm and Passion: *Psalm 31:9-16, Psalm 118:1-2; 19-16,*
                                              Philippians 2:5-11

Your Study Notes Regarding A Preparation for Persecution

What patterns do you observe in the way people react to someone in a place of position or authority? Relate that to the triumphal entry to Jerusalem.

_____

_____

_____

_____

_____

_____

_____

_____

_____

_____

_____

_____

_____

_____

_____

_____

_____

Monday of Holy Week   **Readings: Isaiah 42:1-9; Psalm 36:5-11;**
Hebrews 9:11-15; John 12:1-11

A Peculiar Proof

"Yea though I walk through the valley of the Shadow of Death ...I know you are with me." –Psalm 23:4

After supping with Mary, Martha and Lazarus, Jesus continued His walk to Jerusalem. The miracle of Lazarus being called out from the dead was inflaming Jesus' increased popularity. At this point, amidst their frustration, the chief priests and Pharisees claimed this influence to be the cause of the "whole world" going after Jesus. As this miraculous phenomenon detracted attention from their Temple authority surely they surmised, it potentially could incite a political revolution. Hence the plot was made to kill not only Jesus, but Lazarus too. On the other hand, crowds followed Jesus to Bethany perhaps as they did not want to rely upon the "word of mouth" of this miracle, but rather the "word from the mouth" of the man restored to life! The peculiar proof of this miracle stirred up a great deal of curiosity. But John's account says only that Lazarus sat at the table; there is no suggestion of a verbal testimony. His silenced presence plausibly was a much greater witness.

Lazarus now in his renewed life is freed from the sickness he had endured prior to his first death. His entire existence at this point has been altered radically. So we find a question here about Lazarus that may take us into deeper meditation today. After four days of being dead Jesus called Lazarus out of his tomb. Still bound in grave clothes, is it possible he had to walk through the "valley of the shadow of death" back into life? Consider that death and resurrection for Lazarus was just a shadow at this point, because he would die again and wait for the Resurrection promised "on that last day." A shadow is truly just a reflection of the real thing, an un-illuminated area. F.B. Meyer so puts it that "the shadow of a dog cannot bite... of death cannot destroy." So this death that Lazarus was called out of was not the real thing. Meyer also noted that "you cannot have a shadow unless there be a bright light shining somewhere." Jesus had declared to all that this awakening was for the Glory of God: so that the Son of God might be glorified. Jesus was the Light, reflecting the Shekinah Glory of God! He was the One who would re-establish the real thing –eternal life, in His death and resurrection.

Amazingly, consider that after his miraculous resurrection, Lazarus went back to his home in Bethany, purportedly without any notable fanfare. He awaited Jesus' farewell visits there. Here is a man who had nothing to fear through his walk back into life because the Jehovah-Immanuel, God was with Him! Here is a man who surely felt the laser-like power of the voice that spoke the worlds into creation, speak a new life into his deceased disease-ridden and deteriorated body. Indeed Lazarus bears out as a testimony to the Psalmist cry, "He restoreth my soul!" Out of the chaos of sickness and death, came the transformation of healing. Truly it had to be Goodness –that is God's Grace, and Mercy, that brought Him out of the dark bondage of the grave clothes into the marvelous light. Lazarus's testimony in effect

Suggested Resource: Here are words to a gospel song which also may speak to the message of Lazarus's resurrection and a song for your meditation:

"Your Grace and Mercy, brought me through, I'm living this moment because of You;
I want to thank You, and praise You too: Your grace and mercy, brought me through."
- by Franklin Williams ©1993 Malaco, Inc. (# 270 African American Heritage Hymnal)

could be borne out of that old spiritual song, "*Look where He brought me from...He brought me out of darkness into the marvelous Light, Oh, look where He brought me from!*" It was the unfailing love of his Master and Friend who wept for him, and brought him out of the shadow of death (*darkness*) and placed him under the shadow of the Almighty (*light*). Yet according to John's gospel, there was a peculiar quietness that permeated his presence at the table.

Lazarus resurrection was just the shadow of the real deal. Nevertheless his restoration was needed for the cause that all might believe in Jesus Christ as Messiah. God's ultimate plan would have to be completed. Now all these years later many are still intrigued with similar curiosity just as those who followed Jesus: some people follow because they believe while others follow to stir up theories of skepticism and false claims. Lazarus' raising was a peculiar proof. It was a shadow of what was to come as Jesus indeed was the substance of the true resurrection. Jesus was in essence the real dog that bit death! During these remaining days leading up to Easter we should ask ourselves some questions about what do we believe: Do we believe that Jesus can bring us out of the dark confines of this world's bondage as He brought Lazarus out? Do we believe He can restore to us perhaps a spiritual life that has expired due to the ravages of body and mind? Or even further do we believe He can call us out of sicknesses which no "time release capsule" or "chemo" can cure? Let us pray earnestly in stillness and quiet that Jesus Christ will speak forth in each of our situations of bondage, so as to "Loose *us*, and let *us* go." Let us pray that our testimonies may become peculiar proofs too so that others may believe!

Monday of Holy Week   **Reading: Isaiah 42:1-9; Psalm 36:5-11;**
                                 Hebrews 9:11-15; John 12:1-11

Your Study Notes Regarding A Peculiar Proof

Consider reading John 11 in its entirety for illumination. What new thoughts have you had today about what you believe?

_____

_____

_____

_____

_____

_____

_____

_____

_____

_____

_____

_____

_____

_____

_____

_____

_____

Tuesday of Holy Week   **Isaiah 49:1-7; Psalm 71:1-14; 1 Corinthians**
1:18-31; John 12:20-36

Paradox of the Partition

"How to reach the masses, men of every birth..."Lift the precious Savior up, still He speaks from Eternity: "And I, if I be lifted up from the earth, Will draw all men unto me." -

Dr. William B. McClain in writing the preface to *Songs of Zion* informs us that "the gospel song expresses theology." There have been many worship services wherein the rousing praise of the "gospelized" hymn *"Lift Him Up"* and subsequent renditions of the song have caused many to rise to their feet, and shout to the glory of God. I know I have experienced the exuberant joy of the call and response of "I need somebody... to help me Lift Jesus" which often was elevated to intense pitches of praise. Oh what an experience to feel the power of God's Holy Word being ministered through song and moreover in communion with other worshippers! These experiences perhaps are a type "theology of experience" that Dr. McClain references. High praises, along with the handclapping and the uttering through the lips those words that even Christ Himself spoke, undergirds the praises of a people who over time have struggled in America to not be "proselytes of the gates." [64]

Amid our society and present times we find many people who say "Folks are hungry for the Word." Or as my friend Louise would always say: "Nowadays, people really are looking for something!" What she and many others refer to is that truly many people seek worship experiences which will fill the emptiness that the world inadvertently leaves within. Many seek the ministering of God's Word to warm their spirits within. Some seek a manifestation of the Holy Spirit in their lives to not only comfort and fill them, but also to heal. And some more importantly seek to worship God in "Spirit and in Truth." It is interesting that the John 12 scriptures show us how the "whole world" was moving toward Jesus as He was moving toward the cross. The Greeks as a culture were perpetual philosophical deliberators per se, and "spent their time in nothing else but either to tell or to hear some new thing" (Acts 17:21). So we find as Jesus is headed away from Bethany and the last miracle of His public ministry, there are Greeks, in essence Gentiles, "men of every birth" who seek Him out! When He was born, the wise men sought Him; as He is dying, those who would soon be the beneficiaries of Jesus' "Great Commission" sought Him. They had a likely "point of contact" as Jesus' disciple Philip was noted to be of Greek heritage. What were they seeking?

Were these Greeks like the folks at this present time in our society who are looking continuously for something? Were they hungry for the "Living Bread?" Were they looking for One of whom they heard had done a new thing as Isaiah had prophesied? Or did they want to honor Christ by getting up close to Him?

Jesus knew the price He would soon pay. He knew and confirmed to those who sought Him that the hour for his suffering, death and His glorification had come. By being lifted up on a cross, he signified that His death would be just as a grain of wheat in fertile ground; the fruit of the harvest would yield many souls for eternity; in this case "the multiplying of the redeemed was the magnifying of the Redeemer" [65]

And still today "He speaks from eternity" saying, that "if I am lifted up from the earth, I will draw all men to Myself." He still speaks from eternity when He says God has "highly exalted Him" above all others, therefore every knee shall bow, and every tongue will confess. Oh! What a harvest!!! Jesus still speaks from eternity as he inhabits the praise of our gospel songs if we in "Spirit and Truth" will lift Him higher and higher. And as a result those who still are seeking Him just "may in us the Savior see!"

Therefore as we come nearer to the cross of Christ during this Lenten experience, let us like Philip assist to bring those who are seeking Jesus, and those who desire to see Him close up, into His presence; let us lift Him higher up to those who are looking for something of substance, those who are hungry for His Living Bread. And surely in our praise and worship to the Glory of God, let us give thanks for the lifting of the cross and the veil! And may God please hear our prayer: "Let the world in us the Savior see!"

Tuesday of Holy Week   Isaiah 49:1-7; Psalm 71:1-14 (UMH 794); 1
                                      Corinthians 1:18-31; John 12:20-36

Your Study Notes Regarding the Paradox of the Partition

Why do you think the Greeks represent "all men" in the reading
from John today? How does the phrase "God is no respecter of persons" relate to this reading today?

_____

_____

_____

_____

_____

_____

_____

_____

_____

_____

_____

_____

_____

_____

_____

_____

_____

_____

_____

Wednesday of Holy Week   **Readings: Isaiah 50:4-9*a*; Psalm 70; Hebrews 12:1-3 John 13:21-32**

A Parsimonious Path to Perdition

"Judas hesitated, muttering, "Is it I, Rabbi?" He could have stepped back from the brink, thrown himself on his knees, flung away the thirty pieces of silver secreted on his person and confessed what Jesus already knew." —John Pollock[66]

Judas sat at the table breaking bread and drinking wine together with Jesus and the other disciples, but he would create his own path away from the table. Jesus was distressed as He knew it was Judas, one within His inner circle who would be the culprit to hand Him over to those who wanted to do away with Him. Consider that once the deed was revealed, Judas ran out of the upper room into the night. This was symbolic of the darkness that would lure him down a spiraling path to hell. He had left the table where there was Light. He had left behind the goodness and mercy that could have followed to him for the rest of his life. He had left behind this upper room where Jesus would spend just a few more short intimate moments offering up future compensations and a new commandment of love for those whom God had given him.

Into the night Judas stumbled, as Satan had entered him during the sopping of the bread. What else other than greed made him decide to do this dastardly deal? Maybe Judas was tempted by Satan with similar words as when he tried to tempt Jesus in the wilderness: "All this power" I will give you if you bow down and worship me –easy conditions! Starting with thirty pieces of silver, Satan appealed to his love of money. Perhaps Judas thought he would be given some high office by associating with the likes of Annas, the High Priest and his corrupt sons. Nonetheless, he was being driven by Satan down a path that would cause him ultimately to lose not only the thirty pieces of silver, but also his very soul.

Judas knew Jesus prayed privately in Gethsemane; so this would be the moment he sought to betray Him. "Mingling with the enemies of Jesus," he led the Roman soldiers and lawless crowd to Jesus.

He betrayed him by greeting Him, and kissing him profusely which was suggestive of an intimate kiss of true friendship. Otherwise, the soldiers would not have known who Jesus was. Although Judas had experienced intimate times with the Master, he was not devoted unconditionally to Jesus. What the Word of God does tell us too is that Jesus recognized the act of disloyalty when he questioned him "Judas are you betraying the Son of Man with a kiss?" We learn further however that the act was committed by "the determined purpose and foreknowledge of God."(Acts 2:23) Thus Jesus voluntarily surrendered himself to His enemies. Jesus could have called *"Ten Thousand Angels"* to His rescue, but He chose to drink the cup of death.

Then by morning, just before dawn, Judas realized asking for the thirty pieces of silver was a terrible mistake. At the time he made the transaction with the chief priests and elders he knew that they had no power to pronounce capital punishment upon Jesus. But when in the shadows of the morning Judas saw Jesus being delivered to Pilate, the governor who had no qualms earlier in mingling the blood of Galileans by means of execution, it was at this point Judas wanted out of the deal. He had sold the Master's life for what would be termed in street slang these days as a pocket of "chingle!" His only recourse now was to give back the small change to those scheming rulers of the temple. Except their plot at that moment was just about sealed. They probably laughed in his face as they said no and scoffed at him to handle his own guilt himself! They refused to take the money back which led Judas to disdainfully hurl the coins into the temple. Imagine that he probably heard every piece clink as it hit the marble floors. Blood money it was!

Now Judas was left with the results of the deeds of his wrong judgments. His remorse and repentance however would not lead to salvation. Running away from the temple in despair, He could have pleaded his case before the God of Heaven, such as to implore the thought of: *"When I fall on my knees, with my face to the rising sun, Oh Lord have mercy on me."* Instead he killed himself. The evil had been done; the rulers had used him. Jesus was being marched into Pilate's court. The Sanhedrin had calculatedly manipulated the false witnesses, the truth, the lies, the insinuations, and Judas too, as they rejected Jesus because of their own greed and "stiffneckedness."

Thus we find the scriptural narratives of betrayal and hypocrisy leave us to meditate on the seriousness of the sins of apostasy, greed, corrupt actions, disloyalty, guilt and despair. In our prayers today we should pray for the deliverance of those who would rather not be responsible for injustices committed within our society. Pray for the repentance of those who wash their hands of the truth, and those who are such as a recent news column referred to as "the deaf with hearing ears." Pray as well for those who are lawless and see no significant consequence in the wrong judgments they make. Selah!

Wednesday of Holy Week   **Readings: Isaiah 50:4-9a; Psalm 70; Hebrews 12:1-3 John 13:21-32**

Your Study Notes Regarding A Parsimonious Path to Perdition

Perform a bible dictionary search to understand why Judas was labeled the Son of Perdition.

_____

_____

_____

_____

_____

_____

_____

_____

_____

_____

_____

_____

_____

_____

_____

_____

_____

_____

_____

Holy Thursday   **Reading: Psalm 116:1-4, 12-19; Exodus 12:1-4 (5-10), 11-14; John 13:1-17, 31b-35; 1 Corinthians 11:23-26;**

Praying to Prevail

Lest I forget Gethsemane, lest I forget thine agony, Lest I forget Thy love for me, Lead me to Calvary. [67]

Immediately after instituting the New Covenant that would last forever, there was a song! This dynamic devotion to close out the inauguration of a new Passover nonetheless represented the continuance of a customary ritual – which was to sing the *Hallel* in every dwelling where the Passover was celebrated. [68] What is ironic is the *Hallel* too became the song before Gethsemane, the garden of intense prayer. Included in this particular singing would have been Psalm 116—a thanksgiving for Deliverance from Death!

Recently a pastor from my hometown remarked in an impressive sermon about Jesus' sovereignty, that He had figured out that included among all of Jesus' illustrious attributes, He too was a singer. His cited Luke's deliberate detail to say that after the Last Supper, they sang a hymn as the evidence of this attribute. His remark was a beautiful expression to me. If we revisited in our minds the night of committed agony and betrayal, when all would vow to follow Him to the death, Jesus, divine yet human, took the time to worship through singing psalms of praise. He worshipped the Father in songs of thanksgiving before He would bow down on His knees to pray to the Father in Spirit. He worshipped the Father in thanksgiving as His soul was in turmoil nearing death's door. Historically for the Jews, the singing of the Psalms as a close to the Passover meal also reflected the need for the indebted (those who were passed over in Egypt) out of the depths of their soul to commune with the heart of God.

So on this night after the supper, after the singing, and the walk to the Mount of Olives with His disciples following closely, Jesus would spend a long and emotional night in Gethsemane. Interestingly enough, there is a stark metaphorical parallel of the agony Jesus suffers in Gethsemane as it in some sense resembled the wrestling match Jacob had with God at the Ford of Jabbok. While the two events may parallel in some aspects, there are significant contrasts as well to consider. We know Jesus was blameless and rightfully prophesied as the firstborn of God, yet we cannot say the same for Jacob, as his very name meant supplanter or cheater. He was one who wrongfully gained firstborn status. Jacob needed to contend with God for a new name, because at almost 90 years old, he desperately was in need of transformation. Jesus grappled with God, as He was THE transformation. Jacob encountered God in the form of the Angel, and wrestled with God persistent to receive his blessing yet humbled to weakness. (Genesis 32: 24-32)! Jesus too desperately wrestled in prayer the point of the cup of sorrow he would have to drink, but was obedient to the will of God as He submitted, "Not my will, but yours be done." In this struggle an angel of the Lord then ministered to Him (Luke 22:41), strengthening him to continue His fight. The agony he experienced was a struggle in prayer which caused his sweat to fall to the ground like "great drops of blood!" It would take Jesus all night; but just as Jacob did, he held on! He could not let go of the cup.

With these contrasts of agonizing struggles, I am reminded how the great gospel songwriter Rev. Alvin Darling, a prodigy of the Church of God in Christ penned a great illustration of wrestling and staying power in song. The parallel of the all night struggle in song is driven by a pulsing beat representative of the genre of "good ol' church" gospel sound. Although the music and rhythm are very vibrant, it is still one of those minor key gospel songs that carries the note of sorrow that permeated the cries of our ancestors; a people who too had no other recourse but to "call on the Lord all night long." The minor key music also embodies the struggles of a people who at their lowest points of desperation could commune with God in thanksgiving acknowledging, "I am weak, but thou art strong."

The words and the music might help us understand better a perspective of praying through something. It may be that all these many years past Jacob's wrestle with God and Jesus' desire to release the bitter cup that some of us may need to walk out to a Gethsemane. We may desperately need to labor to the point of exertion (that's what wrestling brings one to) when we need God to speak transformation into and put his everlasting mark upon our lives. The transformation of Jacob's name to Israel would be the foundation for a Jewish ancestral confederacy that still exists today. We will eternally realize the benefits of Jesus' struggle and triumph over Gethsemane. So the *"All Night"* song echoes the strategy on how we should grapple, laboring with God as Rev. Darling wrote:

"All Night I wouldn't give up
All Night I wouldn't let go
All Night I just held on
I called on the Lord all nightlong and I wouldn't let go
Until he blessed my soul. I'm witness that he came through.
Jacob wrestled with the Angel all nightlong and he wouldn't let
go until the break of dawn.
He said, You gotta bless me before You leave.
I felt the same way, when I was on my knees
I asked the Lord to help me to be strong
I called Him all night long.[69]

God honors prevailing prayer. You see we can only witness God coming through on our behalf if we are there wrestling our way through those hardest of times. Preparing our souls for that ultimate time of facing death such as Jesus agonized in Gethsemane is an essential transformation for which we would need to earnestly seek God's will and His face. When earthly friends forsake us, we can pray for God's ministering angels to support us. Wrestling through in worship is one way we can prepare –singing hymns and psalms. We must remember in thanksgiving too as Frank Meyer admonishes us that "Our cup is one of joy, because His cup was one of sorrow. Our cup is one of blessedness because His was one of God-forsakenness." We must not forget Gethsemane. We must not forget this night of agony.

Holy Thursday   Reading: Psalm 116:1-4, 12-19; Exodus 12:1-4 (5-10), 11-14; John 13:1-17, 31*b*-35; 1 Corinthians 11:23-26;

Your Study Notes on Praying to Prevail

Describe some times in your life when you physically were exerted but had to persevere with the task at hand.
List here and Pray today for others you know who need God's ministering angel to attend to them in a time of weakness.

_____

_____

_____

_____

_____

_____

_____

_____

_____

_____

_____

_____

_____

_____

_____

_____

_____

_____

_____

Good Friday   **Readings: Isaiah 52:13-53:12; Psalm 22, Hebrews**
10:16-25; John 18:1-19:42

Presence, Pardons, and the Ultimate Passion

Were you there, when they crucified my Lord?
Were you there when they crucified my Lord?
Oh, sometimes, it causes me to tremble, tremble, tremble.
Were you there, when they crucified my Lord?

Several years ago, while driving alone at night, a melodious sound rang from the car radio. It was a deep and rich toned voice, singing the Negro Spiritual "Were You There?" The singing in progress was just about at the rising point in the song of "Oh sometimes, it causes me to tremble, tremble, tremble!!!" Following that crescendo of the singer's "tremble!" there was then a sudden silence allowing the voice to quietly ease back into "Were you there when they crucified my Lord." An announcer for the broadcast soon broke in amid the ecstatic applause following the singing to say the audience was being blessed by music from Jubilant Sykes, Baritone, at the Moody Bible Institute Founder's Day program. [70] In retrospect, the singing was a most powerful and worshipful meditation in itself.

As the broadcast continued, there was still in my mind a vocalized and piercing question of "Were you there?" Then the next question looming amid the quietness of thoughts was "who was there?" Who was there when they crucified my Lord? Who was there to hear the hammer strike the head of each nail? Who was there to hear Jesus, writhing from the pain and agony of bearing humanity's sins, calling out to His Father, "My God, My God, why hast thou forsaken me?"

Today we remember that day! For the Jews ritually it was a day of the Preparation before Passover which would begin at sunset. But for Jesus and those who followed Him and ministered to Him closely, it was a day to experience and witness tortuous moments and a most excruciating affliction. Early in the morning He was condemned. To the mob's delight, Pilate ordered to have Jesus scourged and delivered up for crucifixion. How hypocritical was it that the Jews as a people who despised the Roman capital punishment of crucifixion yet clamored for Jesus death by crucifixion? The scourging required Jesus to be stripped of His clothing, and most likely he was tied to a whipping post and cruelly beaten, with whips of jagged metal with bone wrapped in a weighted leather thong; this type of beating no doubt would have left his flesh torn. Wounded he was, for transgressions. Bruised He was for iniquities; it was His precious blood that would stream down. Roman soldiers crowned his head with a ring of "thorny bush," then mocked Him as "King of the Jews." Afterward Jesus, the only Son of God, just like Abraham's only son Isaac had to carry the wood for upon which He would be sacrificed. In God's divine and redemptive plan, Calvary was located in the same mounts of Moriah in Jerusalem where that sacrificial ram was trapped.

This was no ordinary criminal's cross although it was treated like one. Moving toward the mount, Simon of Cyrene, an African Jew was forced to help carry the load as Jesus' bruised body was unable to bear the weight of the cross. No, Jesus did not bear the cross up to Calvary alone. It is a wonder to think that Simon was symbolically first in a perpetual line of souls to take up that consecrated cross to bear although he was not the condemned. It was the third hour, nine o'clock when Jesus, truly an innocent Man of Sorrows, was lifted up, suspended between heaven and earth, while flanked by the condemned. It was nine o'clock when He was accused of being "the King of the Jews,"—on this cross a stumbling block for all of Israel!

So who was there at the sixth hour?" After the debauchery, the weeping, and the wailing, the crowd thinned. Many out of fear had abandoned Him; many scurried away as they sensed impending doom with the skies darkening. But John, beloved disciple and first cousin, was still there; the only one of the twelve. Jesus' mother Mary stood there steadfast too. Although her soul at the peak of miraculous divine ecstasy had magnified the Lord God for the great things He had done, she now witnessed and would feel the anguish of the sword piercing; not only through Jesus' body but also her soul. John's mother Salome was there with her sister Mary; an aunt to Jesus. Then there was the other Mary and Mary Magdalene. All who had a loving care for Him were there because of His Love. Those who were obligated to crucify Him as they followed orders of a higher command were still there—these four soldiers ironically would receive forgiveness and mercy undeserved. The hardened thieves, one sarcastic and one repentant were there.

It seems that on that awful day the Lord sat in His Holy Temple! And all of creation stood silent before Him. For all of time throughout the ages, this was the Day that the heavens would rent. For God in His first Person, there could be no communion with sin; He could not look upon His only begotten "Sinner's Substitute" who now took on the sins of the whole world. And although for all of time as the sun had continually run its' appointed course from day to day since creation, this day it could not declare any of God's glory while He in His second Person as the Son would die on that tree. So then we wonder if it was God, in His third Person whose Hand covered the sun so that for three hours it provided a short space in God's eternal time for that evil to subside? And breathing out His Spirit *(last breath)* as it was finished, the testimony shows that the sheer force of Jesus' release tore not only the veil within the temple but broke the crust of the earth causing it to "tremble, tremble, tremble" yielding forth the righteous dead! With that breath Jesus let go of life so that He could gain Life again. God in the midst of this darkness exchanged that crown of thorns for a crown of everlasting glory.

Today is a day of preparation for us too, as we reflect on Jesus' suffering and death! When we encounter others today, knowing we were not there in answer to the song's question, yet knowing what we know, let us be prepared to talk about the deeper things of what happened on and beneath the cross. Let's ask others if knowing what happened at that cross they now have received some new insight? Let's share our passion for His love. Let's tell them of the Love we freely have received and the power of that Love we ourselves have felt. Point them to a wonderful confirmation of faith and new life in God's word such as, *"I am crucified with Christ: nevertheless I live; yet not I but Christ lives in me."* (Gal. 2:20a)

Good Friday   **Readings: Isaiah 52:13-53:12; Psalm 22, Hebrews**
10:16-25; John 18:1-19:42

Your Study Notes on Presence, Pardons and Ultimate Passion

List the levels of pardon that occurred at the Cross and your thoughts about what each meant. Make notes on the how reflecting today on Jesus' suffering may now influence your personal passion for a deeper faith in Him.

_____

_____

_____

_____

_____

_____

_____

_____

_____

_____

_____

_____

_____

_____

_____

_____

_____

Holy Saturday   **Reading: Job 14:1-14; Psalm 31: 1-4, 15-16; I Peter 4:1-8; Matthew 27:57-66**

The Paschal Lamb's Peaceful Position of Power

Low in the grave He Lay, Jesus My Savior, waiting the coming Day, Jesus my Lord...—Robert Lowry

The Hand of God with His Mighty Rod is raised high in the firmament today! He reigns in Victory! With this Rod of Power, wonderworking Power, He signals to all of mankind, "the strife is o'er, the battle done, Alleluia!" As God in the past marched the children of Israel out of Egypt, through the Red Sea, through the barren wilderness of many temptations and hidden enemies, through His Holy Spirit He now has marched through the wilderness entering the gates of Hell victoriously, proclaiming to the inhabitants of Hades to "Lift up your heads O ye Gates" for the "King of Glory" is coming in! "The Lord Strong and Mighty! —the Lord Mighty in Battle" (Psalm 24:7) prevails! With this Rod, He snatches the keys of death and hell, while asking the questions, so "death, where is your sting? O grave, where is your victory?" (I Cor.15:55) Jesus on this Holy Sabbath is beyond the place of the wormwood and the bitter gall (Psalm 69:21). Today Jehovah-Nissi is victorious! Today there is finally a Balm in Gilead! The saints of heaven can echo the Lord's new song of triumph, perhaps singing—"Victory is Mine, victory is Mine. Victory today is Mine!"

We do know that just before the Sabbath and against all legalistic odds, two good men of honor were courageous enough to retrieve and prepare the body of their Master and Rabbi. Hurriedly they had laid Him in a new tomb to "rest and refresh." His redemptive work on the cross was accomplished as He had loved mankind and washed the redeemed past, present, and future from their sins. It was the Blood of this Perfect Paschal Lamb that had made the difference at Calvary. In yielding Himself as the atonement for the past, the bodies of the saints who had fallen asleep were raised. As the atonement for the present, the repentant thief on the cross was personally transported to Paradise. As for the future recompense, Christ would sit at the right hand of God the Father, interceding from a place of power to judge the living and the dead.

So on this day of victory, we find Jesus' times are now in the Hand of the Father God. He here awaits the blessedness of His Spirit powered resurrection and of His ascension to the right Hand of God! The age old question then is brought up in effect amongst those quite like the bewildered women huddled outside of His tomb on this Sabbath, or those who were mourning and trembling with fear at their Savior's death, "Can a man die and live again" (Job14:14)? Nevertheless as of this appointed time, Jesus waits for the change that is to come. The definitive change he awaits is that which he predicted of Himself, "After three days I will rise." Yes, I'll rise again the Master promises. Here we truly understand and know how God's Word cannot return to Him void (Isaiah 55:11)!

Yet the interim change Jesus awaits in the grave is the reversal of the death sentence. The change Jesus awaits in the grave is the call "by the voice of the archangel" to come out! [71] Come out of the linens so painstakingly and lovingly wrapped for His entombment. Come out of the bountifully weighted and fragranced precious ointments and spices He perceived would be His while He sat with Mary and the others that evening in Bethany. Yet from the Gospel accounts we observably find on this Sabbath Jesus is concealed in the grave. We find Jesus is obedient even in death to the fourth and imperative commandment of the Sabbath being a hallowed day of solemn rest, a day of holy convocation (Lev. 23:3). The dawn of the Sabbath found Jesus resting, holding out until His change would come. And is it possible that even a great holy convocation was held in Heaven? Might the "Sons of God" have presented themselves before the throne of God quite like when God declared Job, who was a type of Christ, to be "blameless and upright"(Job 1:6-8)?

ഇൠഅൠ

Note: Hebrew days began at sunset.   Here is an outline according to the way we would view days of the Week during the passion,   crucifixion,   and resurrection of Jesus,

- *Sunset on Thursday was the first day- The Day of Preparation (Friday)*
- *Sunset on Friday began the Sabbath which was the annual day of Passover (Saturday)*
- *Sunset on Saturday constituted the beginning of the third day (Sunday).*

ഇൠഅൠ

Was there a final summit with Moses and Elijah, actuating the Law and the Prophets assent to enthrone the Messiah, King of Glory and secure the Kingdom's power?

Only in the sealed Book of Life perhaps is the key that will unlock the mystery of this Sabbath day. But what we can be assured of is that God, in this process, held up the Banner of Love over all of creation! Think about it, our Jehovah-Nissi still waves this banner of love over the many enemies that wage the guerilla tactics on our lives. These enemies show up in the form of burdens and more that come up against us in times of our own spiritual warfares. They then come out in the open like the people of Amalek did, opposing the purpose and plan God has for our lives; taking on forms such as depression, joblessness, poverty, loss of love, loss of life dear to us; even loss of communion with God. But "thanks be to God for giving us the victory through our Lord Jesus Christ" (I Cor.15: 57) over the enemy and death. As a result we can exchange those thorny problems, concerns, or temptations in our lives for rest and a crown of assurance of hope. We know that we must suffer some things in order to live for Christ. Yet in doing so we must also strive to resolve in our minds to just do that!-Live for Christ. We must not forget however that the world's standard and Christ's standard for the pursuit of happiness stand in total opposition.

Aren't you glad today that God during His Sabbath's rest held up His Mighty Arm and Mercy came running to the front of the battlefield for you and me? Aren't you glad to know Satan is defeated now that Jesus is peacefully positioned as the Holy enthroned King of Glory? We should be glad every time we speak what we believe in affirmation of the Apostle's Creed when we say: "He descended into hell." God wants us to be glad today as we understand Jesus now holds the keys and He also holds the scepter—that wonder-working Rod with which He shall reign forever, and ever! Hallelujah! Hallelujah! *Shalom!*

Holy Saturday   Reading: Job 14:1-14, Psalm 31 1-4, 15-16, 1
                                         Peter 4:1-8; Matthew 27:57-66

Your Study Notes regarding the Power of the Paschal Lamb

How will you prepare for Easter Sunday today? Set aside some time, at least an hour if possible, to position yourself peacefully in God's presence today. Make notes on your experience.

_____

_____

_____

_____

_____

_____

_____

_____

_____

_____

_____

_____

_____

_____

_____

_____

_____

_____

Easter Sunday   **Reading: Mark 16**

In Praise of the Promise: Resurrection Day

"The payment for my sin was the precious gift He gave, now He's alive and there's an empty grave." –Nicole C. Mullen

Early on the morning of the Resurrection, inside of the empty tomb on Jesus' slumber bed laid some neatly folded grave clothes. Even more surprising to those who peered inside was that an Angel of the Lord sat inside there, asking the seekers some benevolent questions. In Mark's account of the exchange, he says the lone angel also tells the women –Mary Magdalene, Mary the mother of James and Salome— "He is risen! He is not here!" This angel then showed them the place where He was laid, and they themselves saw the grave clothes still wound up in the form of the body that had appeared to simply de-materialize away from it.

In Luke's account of these eye witnessed events, the group was asked by two angels in shining garments, "Why do you seek the living among the dead?" We can be sure the angels knew for whom they were looking and why. If they had not been so scared out of their wits, perhaps they should have responded with their own questions of wonderment? But with the sense of alarm and dumbfoundedness amongst the women, each apostle's account agrees that the huge stone was rolled away from the tomb. They agree that Jesus Himself, as they expected Him to be a body only, was not there. So hence their perspective is interpreted that the tomb was empty. Alluded questions of amazement included: "Could someone have stolen His body?" But the angels verified Jesus was alive just as He said. The grief of His suffering and loss made these women and disciples perhaps forget what Jesus had said to them about the third day. With the counsel of the angels they now remember what He said.

Nevertheless, the women were given instructions to go and tell the disciples,—and Peter. Peter was specifically being given a reprieve by the Almighty for his thrice denials of the Savior. Matthew tells us that as the women were going to tell the disciples, Jesus met them saying "Rejoice!" Probably stunned yet overjoyed, they came to His feet, held Him and worshipped Him (Matthew 28:9). Imagine that they may have sung a doxology similar to "Praise God from whom all blessings flow" out of the joy and glory to God. Jesus encouraged the women to "Rejoice" in His resurrection. He asked them to tell the others that the Redeemer lives.

Now we will find all these thousands of years later, songwriters still are composing doxologies of praise to the Risen Savior. One such writer is Nicole C. Mullen, who within the last decade offers us a modern doxology of praise in the words and music of "Redeemer."[72] She sets the stage in this doxology of sort, a gospel ballad however to capture and give glory to the essence of the supernatural things that happened early on that Sunday morning. Although many songs celebrate and praise the resurrection with glorious shouts of acclamation, here we find an inquiry process into the reasoning to understand Jesus' resurrection based on the omnipotence of an Almighty God. You see she touches on some of the questions similarly like ones God may have asked those who questioned His Sovereignty in times long before. For instance, like the questions He asked Job: "Where were you when I laid the foundations of the earth?" or "who [*do you think*] determined its measurements?" (Job 39:2) Or perhaps she was thinking of Isaiah's description of God's greatness when he wrote, "Who has measured the waters in the hollow of His hand...?" (Isaiah 40:12) God even asked Job if he had any understanding of how any of these things even could have been produced. We know Job humbly acquiesced because of the supernatural "almighty-ness" of God that he could not even fathom. So Ms. Mullen simply asks starting her ballad "Who told the sun where to stand in the morning?" however she is moved to proclaim within the song the glory of "now He's alive and there's an empty grave."

So what the women and the others that ran to the tomb on this resurrection morning could not see, or understand was the supernatural workings of a great God. A God who over the annals of time had prepared a dimension of glory divine, which only Christ, the Messiah could take on. It was Jesus now in this dimension which neither we nor they at that time, in our humanness could ever comprehend without Holy intervention. He in a short space of time after

His resurrection mystically would materialize through doors, walls, and even open space along the Emmaus way. He would appear whole in the flesh, not a spirit, but as He was on the cross, with even the marks of the nails that were in His Hands to prove to the doubters it was He. He would appear unrecognizable in the presence of those who knew Him. Only a mighty God could do such miraculous and magnificent wonders. I'd like to think that our African-American forefathers described the glory of resurrection and the phenomena of supernatural, less eloquently in the view of some, yet simply in spiritual terms. They sang "Oh Mary don't you weep, tell Martha not to mourn" because "Pharaoh's army drowned in the Red Sea" as a testament to an Almighty God whose work is supernatural.

So it is no wonder that Ms. Mullen hence more eloquently, affirms in conclusion "I know my Redeemer Lives." Her affirmation spurs us today to give glory for this supernatural act of resurrection. We could choose to look to an authentic doxology of praise in our thanksgiving for the knowledge that Christ lives. This recorded doxology is one we will find to be a true testament to God's Almighty-ness. It doesn't have any gospel shuffle accompanying it, but offers each of us a fitting doxology of praise to a Risen Savior, and the wonders of our Almighty God. The Apostle Paul wrote it this way in the letter to the Ephesians when he proclaimed:

> *"Now to Him who is able to do exceedingly abundantly above all that we could ask or imagine according to the power that works in us. To Him be glory in the church by Christ Jesus to all generations, forever and ever. Amen." (v 3:20 -21)*

Indeed God did more than any could imagine on that third day, that Sunday morning! Jesus got up and left that tomb just like He said He would. God's Glory was thus manifested in a Risen Savior, Jehovah-Jesus Christ, Son of God, Son of Man, "the whole fullness of God," our Lord "infinite and eternal" who is always with us! Who knows, He may be seated right next to you today. To God be the Glory given forever and ever!! Amen!

Easter Sunday   **Reading: Mark 16**

In Praise of the Promise: Resurrection Day
Your Study Notes regarding the Easter Sunday!

So far today, describe any feelings you have experienced as joy on this Easter Day? List some thoughts on how you understand resurrection in context with Easter.

_____

_____

_____

_____

_____

_____

_____

_____

_____

_____

_____

_____

_____

_____

_____

_____

_____

_____

Music Resource for Easter Sunday

God Is Not Dead
(written by Margaret Pleasant Douroux)
(recorded by The Caravans, The Mighty Clouds of Joy, and also
Donald Vails)

Verse 1
If God is dead, what makes the flowers bloom?
If God is dead, what makes summer come in June'
If God is dead, who is listening and answers prayers'

Chorus
I'm glad I know He lives, He lives,
He lives, He lives, He lives, He lives.
I can feel Him moving through the trees,
in the wind, and the breeze.

And I can see Him shining through the night,
in the stars that shines so bright.
If God is dead, what makes my life worth living?
I'm glad I know He lives, He lives,
He lives, He lives, He lives, He lives.

Verse 2
If God is dead, who mends a broken heart?
If God is dead, who keeps night and day apart?
If God is dead, who can tell me where His body lies?

Easter Monday   **Reading: John Chapters 20 and 21**

A Placid Place for Provision and Promise

"When we are most at a loss, Jehovah-jireh." — Matthew Henry

One Easter Sunday morning while driving away from a sunrise service held at the amphitheater near the lake, there was one lone sailboat anchored. It was very still, no movement of the sails or water about it at all. The picture of this was almost haunting yet so serene and so beautiful. In subsequent years, I found many people were sailing or boating up to the amphitheater to participate in the sunrise worship.

Nevertheless, that picture of the solitary vessel perched in tranquil waters, left an etched scene on my mind. The sight of the desolate boat also left a musing question of "Where is Jesus?" as an afterthought on that Easter Sunday morning. It was a suggestive scene of what I thought it was like for the disciples, as Jesus was no longer there to be in the boat with them. Their vessels probably laid anchored out on the Sea of Galilee empty, still, and deserted with the memories of those incredible times seared upon their minds.

Particularly after his forty days in wilderness, so many things happened within or around the boat during Jesus' ministry.

- James and John were in the boat with Zebedee mending nets when Jesus called them.
- Jesus got into the boat to teach and preach to the multitudes
- Jesus often got into the boat to cross over to another location to minister to those waiting or to get to a deserted place by Himself, away from the crowd.
- The Disciples were in the boat when Jesus spoke to the wind and the wave to be still.
- Jesus called Peter out of the boat to walk with Him on the water.
- It was from the boat that the disciples saw Jesus walk on water and worshipped Him saying "Truly you are the Son of God."

- It was from the boat that Jesus came and met a demon-possessed man, who would later beg Him to go with Him, when he got back into the boat.
- It was also in the boat that Jesus often would depart with His disciples to a deserted place by themselves.
- The multitudes that ate the bread Jesus blessed got into boats headed to Capernaum to seek Jesus.
- Jesus commandeered Simon Peter's boat to teach the multitudes and subsequently charged him to let down his nets for a catch unlike any other he had ever had. With broken nets filled with the miraculous catch, Jesus charged Peter from then on similarly he would capture "alive," men.

Now with Word of His Resurrection, the tomb represented a temporary place where the disciples, Peter and John had run with hope only to find empty. Yet within hours of the same day, there would be joy; they would like Adam, the first creation receive the Breath of Life from the Captain of their Salvation, making them into His new creation. Afterward He showed himself to them again in Jerusalem; following that they now would need to wait for Jesus to re-appear to them possibly for a third time. They would need to wait for the promised power from on High.

So it is logical that after His resurrection, and the expectation that He would fulfill His promise to meet them in Galilee, the boat remained a place of consolation for those who had followed Him and His every move so closely. These same disciples were eyewitnesses to many significant events that took place in, near or round about the boat during Jesus' ministry. Particularly in the midst of grief yet with a restrained hope, Peter announced that He was going fishing. Six others of the disciples joined him. They were empty inside and needy of salvation only a Risen Jesus could supply.

Today it is a poignant, near heartrending narrative as we find once more Jesus in His Resurrected body is standing unrecognizable on the shore. So again He commands His Disciples on this same lake from where he first called them, to "Cast their nets "out to the starboard. This early morning appearance would let these disciples know that it was He and His spoken Word that yielded the provision for their miraculous catch. It was the evidence of the weeping that was endured during the "catch-less" night of their despair that now was yielding a "full net" of joy in the morning.

Jesus had promised His disciples that He would meet them in Galilee. He met them where their boats had laid quietly and empty while they were in the midst of their despondency. It is for sure Jesus will meet us where we are in our lives. When we find ourselves tossed and driven on restless seas, when tempests rage about us, or the waves beat into our vessels of life passage, and our own ingenuity fails, we too must look to the shore for Jesus. We must listen for His commands; He urges us to cast our nets to the right side of life's empty promises. As He promised to never leave or forsake us, He is the Light on the life's shore, beckoning us to come and bring our catch to Him. Oh what a blessed assurance God has provided for us!

Today with the joy of having sung Easter songs of "I Serve a Risen Savior...He Lives," or "Christ the Lord Is Risen, Today" still ringing in our minds, let's think about the boat, silently moored in the harbor. Let's consider the wondrous, wondrous work our Lord manifested not only during His ministry from and beyond the boat, but also the wondrous miracle he wrought for His disciples on this morning. John records this narrative for us, so that we might believe. Going forward from this day, let us vow to cast our nets relying only on the power of Jesus our Resurrected Savior and Lord, and believing in Him so that we "may have life in His Name." Amen.

Easter Monday   **Reading: John Chapters 20 and 21**

Your Study notes regarding a Placid Place for Provision and Promise

Where do you need to go from here to further serve Jesus as your Risen Savior?

_____

_____

_____

_____

_____

_____

_____

_____

_____

_____

_____

_____

_____

_____

_____

_____

_____

_____

_____

References

[1] Where Shall I Be? –text by Charles P. Jones- tune: *Judgment Day* 8 4 8 4 with refrain #196, African American Heritage Hymnal, GIA Publications, Inc.

[2] Corinthians 5: -the Message, NavPress, *Copyright © 1993, 1994, 1995, 1996, 2000, 2001, 2002 by Eugene H. Peterson*

[3] *Almost Persuaded* hymn by Philip P. Bliss, 1838-1876

[4] God Is, by Dr. Robert J. Fryson, ©1976; arr. #134, African American Heritage Hymnal, GIA Publications, Inc.

[5] Hymn-*In Times like These* by Ruth Caye Jones, 1902-1972, Tune: 9 9 8 10 D; ©1944 Singspiration Music (ASCAP) African American Heritage Hymnal # 309

[6] Excerpt from *"There's Something about That Name"* Gloria and William Gaither, ©1970 # 171-United Methodist Hymnal

[7] God's Trombones, *The Funeral Sermon* \James Weldon Johnson

[8] Henry, Matthew. "Commentary on Psalms 130". "Matthew Henry Complete Commentaryon the Whole Bible". <http://bible.cross-walk.com/Commentaries/MatthewHenryComplete/mhc-com.cgi?book=ps&chapter=130>. 1706.

[9] Henry, Matthew. "Commentary on 1 Peter 3". "Matthew Henry Complete Commentary on the Whole Bible". <http://bible.cross-walk.com/Commentaries/MatthewHenryComplete/ mhc-com.cgi?book=1pe&chapter=003>. 1706.

[10] O Didn't it Rain, Negro Spiritual *Arr. Harry Thacker Burleigh,©* *1910*

[11] Certainly Lord, *Songs of Zion* #161, Abington Press, Nashville, ©1981

[12] Songbook-Special Songs of...Vol. No. 1-Wards House of Music, Philadelphia, PA

[13] A Theological Introduction to the Book of Psalms: The Psalms as Torah, JClinton Mc Cann Jr., © 1993Abingdon Press, Nashville

[14] No Greater Love © Copyright 1999-2008 by John W. Peterson Music Company. All rights reserved.

[15] The Jameison-Faussett-Brown Commentary, Fausset, A. R., A.M. "Commentary on 1 Corinthians 15". "Commentary Critical and Explanatory on the Whole Bible". <http://bible.crosswalk.com/ Commentaries/JamiesonFaussetBrown/jfb.cgi?book=1co&chapter=015>. 1871

[16] Take up your Cross, Brooklyn Tabernacle Choir, album-Unsorted

[17] New Spirit-Filled Life Bible, page 1365 Mark 8:34-Sacrifice by Fuschia Pickett

[18] Complete Jewish Version Translation Luke 13:31

[19] *The Lord is my Light*, Lillian Bouknight ©1980, Savgos Music, Inc., African American Heritage Hymnal # 160 arr. by Stephen Key© 200 GIA publications, Inc.

[20] Urban Dictionary.com— definition – aka scared: To be afraid or terrified of something or someone.

[21] Scripture References: Matthew 8: 5-13; 9: 9-13; 15:21-28

[22] LUKE 23: *42* Then he said to Jesus, "Lord, remember me when You come into Your kingdom." *43* And Jesus said to him, "Assuredly, I say to you, today you will be with Me in Paradise."

[23] Composer: **Richard Blanchard (1959)**. Meter: 8.7.8.7 with refrain. Copyright: © **1959** Sacred Songs. Arr. ©1971 by Word, Inc. Hymn# 641 United Methodist Hymnal, and #447 African American Heritage Hymnal

[24] *"I Trust In God" by Rev. W.C. Martin*; tune: Charles H. Gabriel Hymn # 144 African American Heritage Hymnal.

[25] Hebrews 11:17-19, The Message by NavPress

[26] New Name in Glory, Traditional African American spiritual, arr Dr. Robert J. Fryson, ©1982 Bob Jay Music Co. # 593 African Heritage Hymnal

[28] Kingdom Dynamics, Gen.17:5- New Spirit-Filled Life Bible, page 26, Copyright © 1982 by Thomas Nelson, Inc., Nashville TN

[29] A Simple Way to Pray by Martin Luther excerpted from The Life and Wisdom of Luther for today by Dr. Archie Parrish, Serve International, Marietta GA 30062www.kingdomprayer.org

[30] Amen! -Traditional Negro Spiritual, #649, African American Heritage Hymnal

[31] Shall we meet Beyond the River, A.M. E. Hymnal #

[32] Come Ye Disconsolate - UMH # 510

[33] "*I Almost Let Go*" music by Kurt Carr, from the album "Awesome Wonder" Copyright © 2000, K. Cartunes, Word Music, Inc.

[34] "This Day" by Edwin Hawkins (Sheet Music - www.ntimemusic. com)

[35] The Wycliffe Bible Commentary, page 14, Copyright © 1962, 1980 Moody Press, Chicago Il

[36] "*We Remember You*" Text by Kirk Dearman, Maranatha Praise Inc. -# 683 African American Heritage Hymnal

[37] John Wesley Writings_____

[38] Speaks, Bishop R.L. Prelude to Pentecost, page 103 ©1985 Wipf and Stock Publishers, Eugene OR

[39] Matthew Henry Commentary on Luke 13, (http://www.biblestudytools.com/Commentaries/MatthewHenryComplete/mhc-com.cgi?book=lu&chapter=13#Lu13_15)

[40] Wycliffe's Bible Commentary, Moody Press, Exodus 20:1-20, page 68

[41] "*Trust and Obey*" –Words by John H. Sammis and music by Daniel B. Towner, #467 United Methodist Hymnal

[42] I Love Thy Kingdom, Lord, 2nd Stanza, Hymn #540 UMH-Timothy Dwight, 1901; music Aaron Williams, the New Universal Psalmodist, 1770; Tune: St. Thomas, Short Meter

[43] *Josephus, the Complete Works*, The Antiquities of the Jews, 3.8.9 v218; page 110, ©1998 Thomas Nelson Publishers, Nashville TN

[44] Frank B. Meyer, The Shepherd Psalm, ©1991 Kregel Publications, Grand Rapids, Michigan

[45] Newton never ceased to marvel at God's mercy and grace that had so dramatically changed his life. *Faith's Review and Expectation* was title from which the hymn Amazing Grace is derived based on 1 Chronicles 17:16-17. Original Poem: "Faith's Review and Expectation" by John Newton, from *Olney Hymns*; Public domain.

[46] *Grace Greater Than Our Sin,* The Brooklyn Tabernacle Choir's "Live…again" CD and Songbook, ©1990 Word Music

[47] *"Here I Am, Lord"* Hymn # 593, United Methodist Hymnal, The United Methodist Publishing House, Nashville, TN

[48] John 3:16, words adapted and music by Jonathan Crumpton, *Shout for Joy! A Soulful Celebration for Easter* -arr. and orchestrated by Dave Williamson ©1998 by Brentwood-Benson music Publishing, Inc. Nashville TN

[49] Look and Live, Text by William A. Ogden, 1841-1897; Tune: Look and Live, 11 8 11 9 with refrain; #503 African American heritage Hymnal

[50] Ephesians 3:20-21

[51] *"At the Table"* by Richard Smallwood ©1999Zomba Songs Inc./ T Autumn Music-Richard Smallwood with Vision, Healing–Live in Detroit, ©1999 Warner Brothers Publications

[52] From the Album/CD *"Alabaster Box"*- CeCe Winans Copyright © 1999 Wellspring Gospel

[53] *"Searching for Heaven on Earth",* by David Jeremiah, Chapter 6, page 57

[54] *"Oh How He Loves You and Me"* from *"Shekinah Glory, Live"* DVD © 2004, 2005 Kingdom Records Music (www.kingdomrecordsinc.com)

[55] Hebrews 2:9- Based on the translation from the Jerusalem Bible, Readers Edition, ©1966, 1967& 1968 by Darton, Longman& Todd Ltd. and Doubleday & Company, Inc.

[56] Contemporary praise-This is the Day!

[57] *"Oh Magnify* (Psalm 34:3)-words and music by Glenn Burleigh ©1993 Burleigh Inspirations Music (BMI)

[58] *"Salvation is Here"* words and music by Eleanor Cooper Brown ©1994

[59] *Jesus Name Above All Names* Naida Hearn,©1974, 1978 (a division of Integrity Music) Mobile AL36685 (source: Praise Worship Songbook 1, Hosanna Music, pg 49)

[60] Quote attributed to Victor Hoagland, C.P.,source: http://www.cptryon.org/xpipassio/

[61] Zechariah 9:9; Isaiah 62:11

[62] Medley of Praise! Maranantha Music, Integrity Music-

[63] Simon of Cyrene was a Northwest African, a Black man, who was compelled by the Roman Soldiers to carry the cross of Jesus up to Golgotha (Aramaic); (Calvary –Latin).

[64] "Proselytes at the gate" is a Hebrew idiom and explains the Greeks/gentiles place in the Temple. The Jews called these proselytes God-fearers. They were Gentiles who came to the synagogue and worshipped God. Although they feared God, the Jews still viewed them as unclean. They could come to the temple but were not allowed to move beyond the outside ring of the temple, called the Courts of the Gentiles.

[65] Matthew Henry's Complete commentary on John 12:23

[66] The Master: a Life of Jesus, John Pollock, pg 176; ©1984, 1985, Victor Books, Wheaton, IL 60189

[67] *Lead Me to Calvary*, Refrain –Jennie Hussey, and William J. Kilpatrick, ©1916, 1944 Hope Publishing Co. Carol Stream, IL 60187

[68] *The Hallel* songs: Psalms 113-118. These songs were sung in two parts: Psalm 113-114, and 115-118. "It is the singing of the second part that is referred to in Matt. 26:30, just before the crucifixion of Jesus."

[69] "*All Night*" by Alvin Darling and Celebration from the album: Recording ©2005

[70] "Jubilant" recorded with trumpeter/composer/arranger Terence Blanchard by Jubilant Sykes. ©1998 Sony Corp.

[71] Matthew Henry's Complete commentary on Job 14 verses 1-15

[72] "Redeemer" from the recording "Nicole C Mullen", ©2000 by Word Entertainment a division of Word Music Group, Inc., Nashville, TN

CPSIA information can be obtained at www.ICGtesting.com
Printed in the USA
LVOW120526171012

303209LV00002B/173/P